Habits of a Healthy Home

Other books by Bill and Nancie Carmichael include

*Lord, Bless My Child: A Keepsake Prayer Journal
to Pray for the Character of God in My Child*

The Best Things Ever Said about Parenting

*Preparing the ground
in which your
children can grow*

Habits *of a* Healthy Home

BILL CARMICHAEL

Tyndale House Publishers, Inc. ● Wheaton, Illinois

Healthy Home Books are designed to strengthen marriages and families by helping to create a home environment that nourishes relationships, builds character, models sound values, and encourages spiritual growth. A Healthy Home—it's what we all desire for ourselves and our children.

Visit Tyndale's exciting Web site at www.tyndale.com

ISBN 0-8423-1490-3

Printed in the United States of America

03 02 01 00 99 98 97
 8   7   6   5   4   3   2

To my children,
who have given me so much love
and have taught me so much
about life and being their dad.

And to my sweet Nancie,
the heart and soul of our family.

CONTENTS

ACKNOWLEDGMENTS

Thanks to Tyndale House Publishers for wanting to publish another parenting book and seeing in this one something unique. And a special thanks to Lynn Vanderzalm, my editor, who puts up with me and continues to do such a wonderful job helping me with my words.

Thanks to Jan Johnson, Ruth Keller, and Nancy Kennedy for their research work. Thanks to Norma Cole and Kathy Boice for their editorial and data assistance.

Thanks to all my pastor friends who have booked me in seminars over the past three years, letting me try out these ideas on their community of believers and get their valuable feedback. Grateful thanks to Earl Book, my spiritual mentor, who has helped me in formulating so many of these concepts over the years of our friendship.

Thanks to my children, parents, siblings, extended family, and friends, who provided the stories in this book. Finally, thanks to my dear wife, Nancie, who has given tirelessly in her feedback about the contents of this book and helped in such a vital way to shape its message.

INTRODUCTION

Having spent the better part of my adult life contemplating and practicing the parent role, not only as a father, but also as the publisher of *Christian Parenting Today* magazine, I have come to the conclusion that *what we do* as parents is secondary to *who we are* as parents.

Some books offer lots of good advice about the various aspects of the parenting process, but the advice often focuses the attention on the children and not on the parents. It tells us how to get our kids to do whatever in ten easy steps. It tends to make us think of parenting as getting our kids to act right and think right. The subconscious message is, "If only you will follow this method, your kids will turn out right."

The danger I see in this approach is that it seems to promise a shortcut to parenting. This approach overlooks the important work of *being* a good parent.

If we as parents are perpetually focused on the behavior of our children, we tend not to look inward at ourselves. We forget that parenting requires as least two persons: a child and a parent. By putting our focus only on our children, we miss 50 percent of the equation.

I find as a parent that it is difficult work to examine myself and change my own attitudes and behaviors so that my children have a good example to follow and a good environment in which to live. This changing-me business is hard work. It is much easier to focus on my children's doings than it is to focus on my being.

If you are looking for a few easy steps to get your children to do the right thing, then this book will probably disappoint you. I leave that to the experts, who are much better than I at giving detailed advice. Rather, this book challenges us to deal with the hard work of *being* godly parents. This book challenges us to reflect about who we are as people and how we can provide a home environment in which our children will grow to be whole, productive, loving, and serving people.

While I was publisher of *Christian Parenting Today* magazine, I talked to or read the letters of hundreds of parents. The most heartbreaking were those who told me they thought they had practiced all of the right methods but their children had rejected most of their parents' values. These parents followed good advice, they read the right books, they held the line, they applied the methods, they disciplined. But when their eighteen-year-old walked out the door, the methods somehow failed to stick with the child. While there are no guarantees and good parents sometimes end up with not-so-good children, I personally have found it very helpful to contemplate the attitudes with which I have applied my own parenting principles. Jesus taught us not just to "speak the truth" but to "speak the truth in love." More careful examination of ourselves as parents and the environment we are creating in our homes can show us that while some of the right stuff is there on the surface, something may be missing at the *heart* of our homes.

I write this book in the hope of helping some parents avoid this heartbreaking trap by taking another look at themselves and the environment they are creating through their personal attitudes and behaviors.

CHAPTER 1

Good Ground

A farmer went out to plant some seed.
As he scattered it across his field,
some seeds fell on a footpath, and the birds came and ate them.
Other seeds fell on shallow soil with underlying rock.
The plants sprang up quickly,
but they soon wilted beneath the hot sun and died
because the roots had no nourishment in the shallow soil.
Other seeds fell among thorns that shot up and
choked out the tender blades.
But some seeds fell on fertile soil
and produced a crop that was thirty, sixty,
and even a hundred times as much as had been planted.
Anyone who is willing to hear
should listen and understand!

MATTHEW 13:3-9

Farming is a tough way to make a living, especially in Montana. My journal entries show the elation and devastation my brother-in-law Dan faced in one painful week of farming. As I see what it takes Dan to raise a good crop of grain, I am reminded of the risks and rewards of raising good kids.

AUGUST 8

It took two days to drive up to Montana to help Dan, my brother-in-law, with his harvest. The days and nights are hot. Through the open window I can hear mosquitoes buzzing against the screen and the hoot owls making their eerie calls from the cottonwood trees that act as a windbreak for the farmhouse. Tonight there is no breeze. The air is dead still.

I think about the times I have been here in the winter, when the wind whips through the fields at fifty miles an hour or more in subzero temperature. I remember the time Nancie and I rode Northern Pacific's Empire Builder up here one Christmas. I wore a synthetic leather jacket, and by the time I carried our suitcases a few feet from the train to my father-in-law's waiting car, my jacket had frozen stiff. One of the sleeves cracked and split as I bent my arm. For a boy from California, it was unbelievable! I wondered why anyone would live here on these windswept plains. It takes an eternal optimist with a passion for farming to stay in these parts.

Dan, a die-hard Swede, loves the challenge of this rugged country. He knows it's hard to get a good crop, especially on these northern plains located only minutes from the Canadian border. There's a lot to fight out here: rocks, alkaline soil, temperatures that can swing as much as eighty degrees in one day, hail as big as rocks, powerful wind, pesky weeds, mosquitoes as big as flies, rattlesnakes, drought that can last for months. A person has to be stubborn to farm this land—more stubborn than the elements. The farmer feels as if he fights some demonic conspiracy against success, and he never knows where or when the enemy will attack.

AUGUST 9

Dan and I drove the fields this morning. The crop looks good. It has had just the right amount of rain and sun this year. Nearly twenty-five hundred acres of land to farm. When the wind blows over the fields, it looks like a gently rolling sea of gold as far as we can see.

"It's just about ready. We can harvest in three or four days," Dan announced. He has been at this all his life, and he knows just by looking at the barley heads that the crop is almost ripe. It will take us a whole month to gather in the entire crop. I can sense that Dan is holding his breath, praying that all will go right the next few days. We greased the gears and tuned the engines of the reapers and trucks. This afternoon we rode the thirteen miles into Conrad for coffee and some supplies.

AUGUST 10

This is the culmination of a year's work and waiting. All the effort, energy, investment, and waiting boil down to a few days of harvest. It is a gambler's dream; the "whole enchilada" is up for grabs, subject to the chance of weather.

Two years ago when I was here to help with the harvest, everything went so smoothly. I remember Dan's absolute delight when the last truckload of grain was safely in the silo. The growing process has to come together just right, and when it does, it's like throwing a touchdown bomb with five seconds left to win the championship game.

Everyone seems a bit on edge. I think we're tired of waiting. Over coffee tonight, Dan and his crew were speculating about the crop. "It could go a hundred bushels per acre, maybe more," Dan had said in a low whisper, as if not to let the forces of nature hear him. As we sipped our coffee, the disc jockey on the local country station said, "I was talking to Doyle over at the co-op yesterday, and he said the crops look good this year all over the county." After a commercial for John Deere tractors, the weather forecaster cut in with sobering words: "Chance of thundershowers tomorrow, but with any luck they should pass us to the north." The farmers around the table looked at each other, sharing their silent apprehension.

AUGUST 11

We saw dark clouds this morning to the north and west. It was not a good sign. By late morning the faces of the men who know these things looked grim. I prayed. By noon the storm arrived, bringing with it hail bigger than marbles. Sheets of it slammed into the waiting stalks of gold like a flurry of machine-gun fire. I watched the hood of the old truck take dents as the hail fell. The proud stalks in the fields twisted, broke, and fell like wounded soldiers. Within five minutes the ground was white with the melting pebbles. In fifteen minutes a year's work lay wasted in the fields.

No one said anything during the fifteen-minute massacre. I looked at Dan, but he just kept squinting at the sky from the bay window. From his expression, I couldn't tell if he was just watching, asking God why, or cursing inwardly. I didn't ask. He's been here before and knows it's the risk he takes. Now his fields may yield only twenty bushels, and some parts of them will just be plowed under, yielding nothing. I feel sick. He was so close. This year is gone.

But the farmers around here keep coming back. Next year Dan will plow, plant, irrigate, pray, and hope. It's hard for me, a city boy, to understand Dan's fierce passion and unyielding tenacity.

GROWING wheat and barley in Montana is a lot like growing a family. The risks can be high, and sometimes life's storms and adversity can thwart even our best efforts. But a faithful farmer like Dan keeps going, knowing that the joy and satisfaction of the years of good harvests far outweigh the disappointment of a damaged crop.

Dan and his coworkers have learned that maintaining

good ground is essential in growing a full crop. While some sections of the fields are more fertile than others, even the best ground needs the care of a skilled farmer. These farmers plow their fields regularly to prevent weeds from springing up and robbing precious nutrients from the ground. They irrigate the ground to maintain just the right level of moisture. And they feed the soil with fertilizer nutrients. Every year the farmers take soil samples from several locations in their fields and send the soil to the agriculture laboratories for analysis. Agriculturists then can tell the farmers what nutrients they need to add for their soil to become good ground. Every farmer knows that without good ground, the crops will fail.

Good ground is essential for bringing up a good family too. Parents who do their part in preparing, tending, and putting the right combination of nutrients into the ground of their families have a much better chance of producing a good crop. Parents' preparation and hard work can make the difference between success and failure when the bad times hit.

But it is not just *doing the right things* that makes good kids. *Who we are as people,* the good earth of our souls, passed on to our children is the most vital component.

The Bible has its own farming story that confirms this. In Matthew 13 we read the story Jesus told about seed and ground. He says that as a farmer scattered the seed, some seed fell beside the path and got eaten by the birds. Some seed fell on rocky soil where the plants sprang up quickly but soon withered and died because they could grow no roots in the shallow soil. Other seed fell among the thorns, which soon choked out the tender shoots. But some seed, Jesus told his followers, fell on good ground and produced a crop that was thirty, sixty, and even a hundred times as much as he had planted.

This parable reminds me of growing grain in Montana and of growing our families. Of course, in the parable we know that Jesus was referring to the Word of God as the seed that is planted in our hearts. But suppose, taking some liberty with the literal interpretation of this story, we picture the seeds as the children God has given us and the ground as our homes. All of the seed was good seed with the potential for growth. The key was the ground. In fact, without good ground, the chances of growing healthy crops—or healthy families—are not very good at all.

We tend to think of children as "good kids," "bad kids," "stubborn kids," "compliant kids," "gifted kids," "lazy kids," "athletic kids," "handicapped kids," or "smart kids." It's easy to slap a label on someone. It's more difficult to see that these little seeds, no matter what type, have a much greater chance to grow roots, develop their gifts, and realize their potential if they are planted in good ground.

This book will explore what makes good ground in which our children can grow. The book discusses issues of the heart. I believe that the essence of healthy homes lies in the invisible spiritual and emotional dynamics by which we live, the hidden rules we practice, and the lifestyle habits on which we stake our lives. Healthy homes that produce good ground are the result not so much of *how we parent* but of *who we are* as parents, as families.

I am truly blessed in that most of my adult life has been spent contemplating and experiencing the parent role. My experience as the founding publisher of Good Family Magazines has allowed me to meet some of the very best family experts of our time. I have attended hundreds of brainstorming and discussion sessions with gifted and caring parents and couples who have shared their hearts and experiences with me.

You would think that this constant wealth of feedback and information would make me the model parent and husband, the father with all the answers and a perfect record in home life. Unfortunately, this is not true.

I remember when I finished my graduate work in educational counseling at the University of Santa Clara, I thought I was pretty well prepared to give expert advice. I recall giving my sister some free advice about how to parent. I did not have any children of my own at the time. But I soon learned that while an advanced degree was a nice background, it did little to prepare me for the realities of raising my own family.

Not only do I often *feel* like a failure as a parent, I have often failed. More than any other factor, our five children have influenced my current convictions about good parenting habits. They have been my best teachers. In fact, it was contemplation about my own performance as a husband and father that led me to write this book.

I have never been much of a fan of how-to methods when it comes to family and parenting. In our editorial brainstorming meetings, I was always the one who chafed against the idea of simple, pat formulas. While these practical ideas are helpful, they do not speak to what makes up the heart and soul of a vibrant, healthy home.

Before starting to write this book, I began to compare the families I met. I started asking some questions: What makes one family a loving, caring unit of people who are bringing up children of purpose and vision, and another family a set of individuals who rarely connect and who have very little direction in life? Is it a matter of income? Is it a matter of schools and neighborhoods? Is it a matter of church affiliation?

I discovered that these factors are not the foundational ones. I met some middle-class families with high incomes, extensive education, and solid church involvement. Yet their homes seemed empty, sterile places, and their children lacked focus. Then I met some low-income families who live in rough neighborhoods with substandard schools and few opportunities for support. Many of these families were led by single mothers. But many of these homes were marked by commitment, and the children had a sense of purpose and vision.

If financial stability, education, and church involvement do not account for the difference, what does? What are the foundations of a healthy home? Everywhere Nancie and I went to do one of our family seminars, we asked parents what they believed to be the basic ingredients of healthy homes, of good ground. We asked hundreds of people. The same answers seemed to emerge. *Turning out good children is not something we do as parents; it is an environment we create.* Healthy homes concentrate more on the *why* than the *how*.

This book is about the things we all know—or at least assume we know—about home. They are the things we take for granted, the things that often become most important. They are the things we return to when we finally stop long enough to add up our real assets. They are what most of us know almost instinctively, the eternal truths that can be found somewhere deep inside our hearts and souls.

The truth is, home is the stuff of everyday living. It is always a mixture of good and bad, joy and sadness, pleasure and pain, rights and wrongs. But in the end, for most of us, it is the place where our hearts return, and we remember its solace, its comfort, its hearth.

The ideas in this book are spiritual in nature; that is, they have a bigger-than-life meaning that cuts to the heart. You will find them rooted in age-old biblical principles. My attempt is to reaffirm the idea that what you know about home—what you dream, what you feel when the feelings are good, and what we all want—are the things to follow. And if we follow them, we will find contentment and joy and will bring up good kids who know how to hope and cope.

What is the good ground of your home and of mine? Is it possible to take some soil samples from our homes and know how to put the right ingredients into the ground? I think it is. The good ground of our homes will provide solid answers to some basic questions we all have about life:

1. Am I safe?
2. Who am I?
3. What are the rules?
4. Is life good?
5. Am I loved?
6. Where do I belong?
7. Why am I here?

I believe that to answer these questions, a healthy home must be a place of *refuge,* a place of *formation,* a place of *boundaries,* a place of *celebration,* a place of *connection,* a place with a *legacy,* and a place with *purpose.* In the end, it's the soil, the environment of home, that makes it happen. *Refuge* provides the place and lets us know we're safe. *Formation* provides the virtues and gives us tools to become. *Boundaries* provide the context and let us know the rules. *Celebration* provides the joy and lets us know that life is good. *Connection* provides belonging and lets us know we're loved. *Legacy* provides the roots and lets us know from whence we came. *Purpose* provides the reason and lets us discover our calling. The remainder of this book will explore each of these seven habits of a healthy home.

Note that these habits are not things we *do* but are the essence of who we *are.* Like the makeup of the soil, these habits are the stuff of which we and our homes are made. They are the stuff of *being,* not doing.

We are all aware of the nostalgic myths of home and family, images that usually seem better in memory than they were in reality. I know there is no such thing as a perfect home. It has been painful for me in looking back to discover that I unconsciously did some things that fostered just the opposite of what I want to see in my children. I believe I am a good parent, but even good parents fail and foster the wrong environment.

Take comfort in knowing that we all bring the baggage of the past into our homes. All of us have been wounded and tend to pass on those wounds to our children. We all struggle with bad habits and traits. Sometimes we kid ourselves and think that somewhere out there are parents with perfect kids who automatically grow up to make their parents very proud. Well, we can relax because the myth of the perfect family is just not true.

The seven habits discussed in this book are *ideals* for us to aspire to and reach for. They will become more natural and more consistent as we take them into our hearts and value them as essential things we wish for in our personal lives.

HOME is the soil in which we are planted. Let's do what we can to create good ground, better ground, in which our children can take root and become sturdy, productive plants. Just as my brother-in-law Dan fights for each year's crop, we must see our homes as worth fighting for, worth improving, worth pulling up to a new standard of hope and goodness.

The following thoughts and stories about what makes our homes good ground come from the grateful heart of a pilgrim family "farmer" just like you.

CHAPTER 2

Refuge
Am I Safe?

Those who fear the Lord are secure;
he will be a place of refuge for their children.

PROVERBS 14:26

🌿 "I'm Home!"
A man travels the world over in search of what he needs and returns home to find it.

GEORGE MOORE

I DON'T know why the old farmhouse in Clifton, Colorado, stands out from all the houses my family lived in, but something about that time in my life seems to carry a special memory. Maybe it's because I remember it as the house where, when Uncle Laverne visited us one summer, my mom accidentally walked in on him in the bathroom while he was getting out of the tub, stark naked. They both screamed, and nothing much was said after that. I went to my room and laughed until my twelve-year-old sides ached. That's a vivid memory, but I think I would've remembered that no matter where we lived. No, there was something more about this place where we lived for less than a year.

When I was in the seventh grade, my father decided to move from California to Colorado. It was the early 1950s, and atomic power was thought to be the energy source of the future. My dad, ever the entrepreneur, decided the uranium-ore mining boom was a great opportunity to get rich. My dad was not a miner; he was a builder. But my father surmised that with all the flurry of new uranium mines in Colorado, there would be lots of construction going on. A friend who lived in Grand Junction convinced my dad that we should move there, so off we went.

We rented an old farmhouse in the middle of a peach orchard. The house was grand. It had a big, screened-in front porch with strong pillars supporting the entryway. On hot summer nights the front porch was the perfect place to sleep. The living room, with wood floors and a calico throw rug, had a large brick fireplace with a sturdy mantel painted white. Big overstuffed chairs surrounded the fireplace. It was the warmest place in the house.

The old country kitchen was white and yellow, with a blue flower wallpaper on the south wall. On sunny mornings the warm light burst through the dining area that faced the old red barn and a chicken coop. My sister, Charlene, had her own room. My little brother, Jimmy, and I shared a big room with bunk beds. He slept on the top because I told him he had to.

In the summer at this place, ripe, golden peaches hung heavy, almost touching the soft ground beneath. There is nothing so delightful, so sweet and juicy, as tree-ripened Elberta peaches in the middle of July. I learned how to rub the fuzz off a fresh peach and eat it whole, like an apple. We had peach pie, homemade peach ice cream, peach cobbler, peaches and cream, and peach jam, as well as peaches on cereal, pancakes, and waffles. We canned peaches in a big kettle on our kitchen stove. Mom's hair stuck to her face from all the steam. You would think I would've gotten sick of peaches. Mom did, but I never did.

Behind the farm was a lazy canal that I thought had been made just for me and my brother. We shared our swimming hole with muskrats and mud hens. It was heaven for a twelve-year-old boy and his nine-year-old brother.

This old farm had character and adventure. It was different from the other places we had lived. Most of the other houses were new ones my dad had built in subdivisions, and they all sort of blend together in my memory. But this grand old farm is one of my best memories of home.

And yet as I reflect on this place, I don't think it was the house and farm as much as it was a moment in time for my family. For me, it had all the qualities of refuge. I was twelve, old enough to seek adventure but young enough to be a child. Jimmy thought I knew everything. My parents seemed contented. My sister was sixteen and in love with the boy she eventually married. We were together, we had enough, and we were happy. Life was simple. Life was good. My parents tell me we were dead broke then, but for all I knew, we had plenty. Our "ground" was rich with elements of tranquillity and contentment. We simply loved each other for who we were at that moment of time. It was the best of times because I felt loved and secure.

Your experience is different from mine, but perhaps you can think of a childhood time when life was easy and all was well, when you didn't crave for better or more, when you were contented, when you knew you were loved.

What made it a refuge for us? Open arms. Hugs. A listening ear. Unconditional love. Attention. Our own space. People who adored us with their eyes. People who cared, who were attentive to the little changes in our countenance and voice inflections, who stroked our heads, kissed our cheeks, and fixed our favorite foods at just the right times when we needed a boost.

We all need a place of refuge, a place of peace, a retreat from the noise and fast pace of life. The need is burned deep within us. We need a place to find solace, a harbor from the storms of life, a place that rekindles our soul and gives us hope in ourselves again.

Home can be for us a refuge, a place to belong and to be loved, a place that accepts us, binds our wounds, and rejuvenates our spirit. Home is people who cuddle us and encourage us, defend us and support us in our grief. It is not a perfect place; we are human, after all. But it is a place with familiar sights and smells, a place where we can let down our guard, set aside our assumed roles, do away with pretenses, and be ourselves. It is a place of grace, of forgiveness. It is a place where memory gathers. In this place, I am welcome. I am safe.

The idea of refuge is not a mystical concept; it is an attitude of the heart. As poet Robert Frost wrote, "Home is the place where, when you have to go there, they have to take you in."[1] Home is the place we envision will always be there for us, and it is what we long to create for our children.

We parents are the ones who create this atmosphere of refuge. Home as a refuge is not a street address, not a zip code; it is people who care. Making home a place of refuge for our children is an important habit. The sense of refuge and safety that home can give to our children will go with them through their entire lives. Throughout our lives, this childhood experience of refuge is the memory bank in which

all other deposits are made. Nothing will be discovered in our
lifetime to replace home as our safe place. My home is my
story. My home is my life. My home is me. When they feel
loved and secure, our children will be able to say those two
wonderful words: "I'm home!"

🌿 Home As "Place"

All the places we have lived in remain with us,
like the pegs in a vast storehouse, on which our memories are
    hung.
They symbolize all the states of mind through which we have
    lived,
with all their varied shades of feeling.
PAUL TOURNIER

"PLACE" is an essential part of knowing who we are. It
gives us and our children the roots to form new places as our
life goes on. "Place" is the people, locations, and things that
combine to give us a sense of refuge. It is a basic component
of good ground.

My father had a restless gypsy soul. He was a mover.
When I was a kid, we lived in thirteen different houses, in five
different towns, in two different states. I went to eight different schools before graduating from high school. Considering
that I lived in the same house until I was eight years old and
that I graduated from high school when I was seventeen, we
averaged a move more than once a year during the nine-year
span from third grade until my high school graduation.

My father was a house builder, and as soon as he finished
a new house, we would move. Our houses nearly always had a

For Sale sign out front. Because of our family mobility, home for me was not always a "place" in the sense of a specific location. Instead, "place" became familiar things, like my pine dresser with the little gray-and-white rabbit skin under my lamp. The rabbit was one I had shot while hunting with my father, and I had skinned it and tanned it myself. "Place" for me was my little wooden desk with small beads of dried glue left over from building plastic models. It was the collection of little things I kept in my drawer—a Willie Mays baseball card, a picture of me playing in the snow when I was about seven, a small red portable radio with earplugs, and a set of Golden storybooks.

"Place" was my mother's cooking—the same recipes and smells no matter where we lived. The memory of coming home from church to the smells of pot roast with carrots, onions, and potatoes baking in the oven is still deliriously wonderful.

"Place" was made of my yellow bedspread, my old soft pillow, my 1940 army-issue wool blanket, my mother's "Desert Rose" dishes. These portable things became my home. "Place" for me became the things I could take with me, things easily mobile and transportable.

Nancie's childhood experience of "place" was very different from mine. She lived all her life in the same Montana farmhouse until she left for college. Her brother still owns that farm. She spoke of "place" in a way that was foreign to me. I did not understand her attachment to a location, to a plot of dirt, to rooms and old barns.

The beginning of our married life was in my tradition. We moved from San Francisco to Santa Clara to Santa Cruz to

Albany to Springfield to Salem. During the first few years of our marriage, we lived in eleven different houses or apartments in eight different towns located in two states. And then we moved into the house we still live in today.

For the past seventeen years, we have lived Nancie's tradition in a place in central Oregon. We moved here when Jonathan, our oldest, now twenty-seven and married, was beginning fifth grade. We built this house in the ponderosa-pine forest with our own hands. I sketched the drawings and completed the house plans. My dad and I drove many of the nails in the framing. I picked out each wood window from the factory. We gathered the rocks in the mountains near our home and directed the mason, stone by stone, in building the huge rock fireplace that sits in our open-beam living room and dances with warm fire on snowy winter nights.

We built the decks, adding on several over the years until now we have a deck across the entire back of the house, with lazy cedar Adirondack chairs for lounging on hot summer days. It is really our house in every sense. I never understood attachment to a specific place until this house.

I love this house. It is so familiar. Its corners and angles, its rooms and windows, its wood and rock, its squeaks and whirs are all so predictable and familiar.

Years ago we bought the biggest dining-room table we could find. With all the leaves in it, the table can seat twelve. Countless meals and games have seen the faces of our family and loved ones around that table. That table has witnessed some of the best times we remember as a family.

Several trees in our yard have grown up with our children and are growing old with Nancie and me. I sometimes walk out the back of the house and stare back at its angles, wood, and windows. When the light shines on the deck and walls on an early summer morning, the house is the most beautiful place I have ever seen. It is our castle. It is wholly ours. The other day I calculated that this house contains the memories of over 6,235 days together as family, a giant scrapbook of memories in every room. I did not know it was possible to feel this way about a place until we built this house.

I am not attached to this house for its material value. I do not love it for its ornate elegance; it doesn't have much of that. It has little in the way of gold fixtures or stained glass. It has no fine art on its walls. It is certainly not the most expensive house in our neighborhood. But it is our family refuge, our place. It is where the memories of our family reside. It is safe. This house has personality and soul.

Remember that home as "place" can happen even if you are in a mobile family like my childhood family. Even though I moved frequently as a child, I had a sense of "place" because of the people and things that took the sojourn with me. This really is all that our children need to sense refuge.

"Place" can happen in any location. I have visited African mud huts with manure floors and thatched roofs and have felt a sense of "place" for the family. "Place" means having the space that is yours, with people who care.

Jesus spoke of "place" in one of the most comforting and hopeful passages of Scripture. He told his disciples, "Don't be troubled. . . . I am going to prepare a place for you. If this were not so, I would tell you plainly. When everything is ready, I will come and get you, so that you will always be with me where I am."[2] During the last days of his life on earth,

Jesus was preparing his disciples to live without him. These were men who had left their occupations and homes to follow Jesus. Now he was going to leave them. Wanting to muster hope and courage, Jesus did not give his followers a pep talk. Instead, he did a more powerful thing; he spoke of going to prepare a "place." It was exactly what they needed at that moment—a sense of refuge, a sense of hope.

Think of how energy-consuming it would be to have no stopping place, no place where you felt safe. It is an awful thing to imagine how "place" has been desecrated for children of war-torn places like Vietnam, Cambodia, all of Europe during World War II, and Bosnia more recently. It is hard to imagine the uprooting, the loss of the familiar, the destruction of feeling secure. For them, home base was destroyed. There was no place to hide, no place safe. It is an essential human need to have a "place" that is our own.

We must sanctify our homes to make them places of hope, love, and healing. "Place" in this context means that our homes become sanctuaries, sacred places. They become places of quiet and solitude, of comfort and joy, of prayer and devotion, of spiritual renewal.

🌿 Am I Safe?
If the child is safe, everyone is safe.
G. CAMPBELL MORGAN

WHEN I was seven, I had a best friend named Corky. Corky lived in a house with a large front yard bordered from the street by a waist-high white picket fence. Small as it was, it was our neighborhood's favorite baseball field.

One day stands out from all the rest. I was at bat. Corky pitched me the ball, and I hit one of the best hits of my life. The ball went over the white picket fence, across the street, under the hedge, and into the yard of David and Danny Hernandez. David and Danny, thirteen and fourteen years old, were the neighborhood bullies. They did not like us smaller children cluttering their neighborhood, and they certainly didn't like us entering their yard.

My elation over smacking a home run soon turned to a discussion about who would be the one to retrieve the ball from David and Danny's yard. The first suggestion was that since I had hit the home run, I should retrieve the ball. My suggestion was that since it was Corky's ball, he should go get it. Finally, we agreed to play rock-scissors-paper in order to determine to whom this grim task would fall. The lot fell to Corky.

We all watched quietly as Corky crossed the street and peered around the corner of the thick hedge hiding David and Danny's house. Then he disappeared as if to make a dash for the ball. Suddenly we heard his scream. I heard the deepening voice of one of the bully brothers curse Corky. Corky let out another agonizing yelp and came running around the corner of the hedge. David was dragging Corky by his red hair, and Danny was kicking him as they moved into the street. Corky was moaning and crying, his freckled face beet red, snot running out his nose, and tears of terror streaking his dirty cheeks.

A mixture of fear and anger clutched my stomach. Corky was my best friend, and from the look on his face and the guttural sounds he made, I thought he would be killed. I had to do something. Without a thought to the consequence, I picked up a large clod of dirt from the flower bed bordering Corky's front yard, ran toward the street, and hurled the clod as hard as I could at David. He was looking down at Corky at the instant it hit him. *Smack!* A direct hit, right on top of his head. A puff of dust and little brown clods flew everywhere.

David's head snapped up, and the eyes that met mine showed fire and death. He dropped Corky and lunged for me just as I sprinted down the sidewalk. My house was three houses down, and I put my little legs in motion as fast as I could make them go, past Louise Dockem's house, toward Orval Schenkowski's house. David was now gaining on me. I could hear his footsteps and cursing as I passed Orval's house and turned sharply up my driveway toward the back screen door that I knew was unlocked.

David was now so close that I could hear his labored breathing. I knew that if he caught me, my life was over. He reached out to grab my shirt just as I grabbed the handle of the screen door of my house. I heard my shirt tear as I stumbled into the back porch of my house. The screen door slammed behind me. I reached up and fumbled for the latch, but David did not try to come in. He stood panting and cursing just outside my door. Even an uncouth primeval bully like David knew some basic law of privacy that said he could not trespass the sacred domain of another's house. When I had been out there, on the other side of the screen door, I was fair game. But once I was inside my house, I was safe.

MOST of our experiences are the "out there" kind. "Out there" is comprised of the places—school, work, the neighborhood, church—that are not home. Adults and children receive all kinds of challenges and threats out there. Competition, attacks on self-esteem, peer pressure, demands to perform, and the pressures of the pecking order all require an emotional energy that we can't sustain if we don't have a retreat place where we can feel safe, where we can let down our guard and be vulnerable. That is why it is essential for most of us to feel we have a safe place to unravel and where our emotional batteries can be recharged.

Journalist Charles McDowell captured the feeling of safety when he compared running toward home plate in a baseball game with coming home in real life.

> The idea that home plate has a little roof—a little roof—it's a little house. It brings us back to where we're safe and where we care and where we are cared about and where we are loved.
>
> Coming home on a baseball diamond is pretty . . . dramatic. You feel relief to have gotten out of all those hazards out there. Between first and third is hazardous territory. And then third to home is joy! You're out of trouble. You're coming back. And you're running toward the home team dugout. You can see [your coach and teammates], and they're all grinning. They're glad to see you, and their arms are out. And you come across home plate. It's pretty Big League stuff.[3]

Sometimes, unfortunately, the threats and hazards to children's sense of safety come from *within* the home. That was the case for Michael.

It had been over forty years since the ordeal ended, but when Michael told me his story, the pain was still evident. Michael came from a loving and stable home. But there were times when he did not feel safe. Michael knew his parents loved him, but he also knew he frustrated them. He was a strong-willed child with a streak of wild creativity and maverick curiosity that was difficult for adults to understand and channel. His teachers used to tell his parents, "Michael seems to think there is a special set of rules just for him."

"I got a lot of spankings as a kid," he told me. "It was the only way my parents knew how to discipline. In those days, a good licking was the way to deal with misbehavior, at least in my home."

Then Michael told me about his bed-wetting, the behavior that seemed to be the focus of his parents' frustration with him. His parents were concerned that this behavior was eroding their son's chances of a normal life. Michael said they tried everything to get him to stop wetting the bed. "I do not ever remember sleeping without a rubber sheet covering my mattress until I was about fifteen years old," he said.

During Michael's childhood, he was never able to spend the night over at friends' houses. "I had to make excuses at Cub Scouts as to why I could never go on the overnight outings."

"When I was about seven years old," Michael said, "my mother decided that putting me back in diapers was not only practical but also might be the key to getting me to stop wetting." She used large dish towels for diapers. Michael said he remembers aunts, uncles, and even some friends seeing him in diapers. "I was humiliated by this experience," he said. "I began expressing my anger by being a bully to my younger sister and some of the smaller neighborhood kids. My performance at school hit a downward spiral."

When Michael was about eight or nine years old, his parents read about an alarm system made up of two metal screens placed on either side of cloth bedsheets. When the sheets became wet, a buzzer would wake the child. "My mother tells me that the alarm would go off five or six times a night. Needless to say, this prevented my parents from sleeping and further frustrated all of us."

Michael's parents decided to try spanking. They stored the buzzer contraption, and every day for several days Michael's father gave him a spanking for wetting the bed. The wetting continued, and the spankings stopped.

Once again Michael's parents tried the buzzer contraption. The metal screens had corroded, so Michael's father made some copper screens to place under his sheets. While the changes were intended to fix the system, these homemade screens had another surprise.

"Copper mixed with urine has a corrosive and toxic effect on human skin," Michael told me. "After a few nights, huge red rashes began to form on my thighs and legs. Soon my body was covered with large oozing sores. My mother bought some ointment, and my parents stopped using the contraption," he said.

Eventually his legs healed, but the frustration for all of them continued. Michael's parents believed that he could control his bed-wetting if he really wanted to.

Bed-wetting permeated every aspect of the relationship between Michael and his parents. While Michael can now see the frustration his parents felt and recognize the labor of love his mother performed in washing the sheets for so many years, he feels that the intensity with which this problem became *the* issue hurt the relationship.

During Michael's early teens, wetting became less and less frequent, and one day when he was fifteen, it stopped. But the chasm created between Michael and his parents left him feeling unsafe for much of his childhood. It was not until years later that both he and his parents understood that this was a biological problem, something Michael could not help, and some emotional healing took place.

Even good and loving parents can inadvertently rob their children of a safe environment. Michael's parents bored in on one frustrating behavior with machine-gun force, demanding change. They saw their frustration more clearly than they saw their son's pain. Their intent was good—to rid themselves and their son of this unwanted blight—but in doing so, they caused Michael to feel unsafe in his own home every night.

I confess that I also have occasionally made my children feel unsafe. When I became a father, I found things that frustrated me. I remember wanting them to like vegetables, and I made Jon sit at the table for hours one evening until he ate some fresh cucumbers and tomatoes his mother had prepared. To this day, Jon hates fresh cucumbers and tomatoes.

I wanted my kids to be normal, to fit in. I wanted them to excel, and I certainly wanted them to behave in a way that pleased me. When their behavior did not please me or when they told me what I did not want to hear, I sometimes created an atmosphere that felt unsafe for them. I raised my voice. I sometimes showed anger or frustration when confronting my children. When children have to use lots of emotional energy in an attempt to maintain vital relationships with family members, they can feel their sense of safety eroding.

Sometimes in living the daily routine, we parents forget that we give unsafe messages to our children in very subtle ways. Our tone of voice, our methods of discipline, the moods in which we discipline, and the nonverbal messages we give off can signal children that they may not be entirely safe. Children often interpret our frustration and impatience as their fault, their flaw.

What does a safe place feel like? Essentially it is a place where we don't have to give out a lot of emotional energy to maintain our existence. It's a place where we can be vulnerable and not be penalized for it. It is a place where we do not have to compete. It is a place where we feel loved and accepted without having to try. To feel safe means that we feel loved and accepted first, corrected and admonished second.

We make our children feel safe in the same ways we feel safe—by giving them space, by not probing, by loving and listening with acceptance and advocacy, by indulging them at times when they need it.

As parents it is easy to focus on our own needs and agendas. We see our children brooding, and instead of lovingly drawing them out to discover and help them with their pain, we tell them to snap out of it. Sometimes we focus on the behavior we don't like rather than try to discover what emotions or feelings may lie behind the behavior. We want to talk our children into right behaviors rather than listen and love our children into right behaviors. Children feel safe when they do not have to spend lots of emotional energy maintaining their sense of self.

We have all heard the alarming statistics indicating that child abuse is on the rise. It is painful to know that thousands of children go to bed every night with bruises—both physical and emotional—because parents can't control their rage. Physical, sexual, and emotional abuse of children is a most devastating crime precisely because it most often comes from someone whom the children expect will protect and defend them. The shame, confusion, and emotional wounds given to abused children are beyond words. If you are an angry parent, if the rage inside of you is sometimes uncontrollable, I beg you to seek professional help before it is too late. If you care about the well-being of your children, talk to someone now.

And even if you do not consider yourself an angry or abusive parent, ask yourself whether your children feel safe in your home. Ask yourself, "Do I focus on an agenda of right behaviors and conformity, or do I focus on loving and listening to my children?"

Our children have a right to feel safe at home. Competition, danger, risk, and abuse are plentiful "out there." These should not be part of a child's sanctuary. Home should be a place that says, "You are safe in my presence. You are safe in this place. Your sense of self-worth will be protected in this home."

Am I Accepted?

We are born helpless.
As soon as we are fully conscious, we discover loneliness.
We need others physically, emotionally, intellectually;
we need them if we are to know anything, even ourselves.
C. S. LEWIS

MAKING refuge a habit in your home also means giving your children unconditional acceptance. Acceptance is a powerful human need. Where we are accepted, we can feel safe enough to be vulnerable. In an atmosphere of acceptance we can open up and tell others who we really are and how we really feel.

Nancie and I adopted our daughter, Amy, from Korea when she was three. As I look back, she must have felt as if she had been captured by aliens. She was whisked away from her homeland on a jet, only to arrive in a strange country where people looked different, spoke an unintelligible language, and ate odd-tasting food.

Amy is now in eighth grade. I heard her come home after school one day recently. She went straight up to her room, saying nothing, even though I yelled a greeting. I knew then that something was wrong. I waited for a few minutes, busy on my word processor.

Soon she came down the stairs and into my home office. Without looking up from my work, I said, "Hi, honey. Did you have a good day today?"

She slid down the wall until she was sitting on the carpet. When I turned to look at her, I noticed she had been crying. "The first part of the day was okay. . . ." She couldn't finish. Bursting into uncontrollable sobs, she crawled to her feet and scampered out of the room. I followed, finding her in the living room in heaving sobs.

I sat beside her and took her in my arms as she wept. Finally, after several minutes she said, "I had to hold my tears all day, Dad."

"What happened?" I asked. Through her sobs she told me. We were unaware that every day at school, a group of boys made fun of her ethnic features. When they passed her in the hall, they pulled at their eyes to make them look slanted. Often they teased her by speaking some kind of gibberish, making fun of what they think sounds like an Asian dialect.

We live in a small town where she is the only Asian-looking child in her junior high school. All of us remember the agony of junior high, how we desperately wanted to fit in, to be like our peers, feeling terribly self-conscious about every little thing. Imagine being the only Asian in the entire school. Imagine having your differences mocked every day. Then add to this the fact that Amy has learning disabilities that prevent her from keeping up academically with her peers. Get the picture?

On this particular day, Amy went over the edge. After keeping her composure for nearly four months, she reached her limit. She held in her tears on the bus and in front of her peers, but once she was safe at home in an atmosphere of acceptance, she could let it all out. "I never want to go back to that school, Dad," she said through gasps and sobs. "Can't we move and find a school with at least some Asians in it?"

I told her we would discuss it with her mom when she got home. I also told her that God must have something very special for her because anyone who had to go through what she was going through would come out with tremendous compassion for the disadvantaged and downtrodden. I told her that sometimes life isn't fair and that people can be very cruel. I told her that two-thirds of the world looks more like her than they do like me and those insensitive boys. I also told her that if I could, I would go and punch those boys' lights out! That made her smile. They were not very good words, but they were the best I could think of at the moment. We hugged and prayed. I told her I loved her very much.

I know at that moment Amy felt completely accepted and safe. As we clung to each other for a few silent moments, I felt the grief she was feeling, and she felt my unconditional acceptance of her. In a sense, her grief flowed into me while my love flowed into her. It was a moment of refuge she desperately needed.

How we communicate with and relate to our children tells them whether or not it is safe for them to be vulnerable with us. Children feel accepted when we say things like, "I think I understand why you feel the way you do," or "Help me see this from your point of view." Conversely, children feel insecure when we hold out to them an unending array of "shoulds" and "oughts" and "musts." "You shouldn't feel that way," or "You ought to feel happy," or "You mustn't be so foolish." In an environment like this, the child's honesty is diminished and judged to be unacceptable.

Henri Nouwen said, "A little criticism makes me angry, and a little rejection makes me depressed. A little praise raises my spirits, and a little success excites me. It takes very little to raise me up or thrust me down."[4]

Home is the one place where we need to receive unconditional acceptance just for being who we are. Every family has its members who are a bit different. Mine certainly has. It's helpful to remember that different does not mean *wrong* or *bad;* it just means *different.* Even the most difficult people in our circle need a place where they can be understood and forgiven. All of us need somebody who helps us get a fresh start.

We parents are in a unique position to help our children to feel valued. When we listen to them, adore them, and take pride in them, we help them feel accepted.

🌿 Honoring a Child's Privacy

If we have no privacy, we lose our identity: It is swallowed in the mass.

We do not know who we are even if we are celebrities and everybody on earth knows our name.

LEWIS SMEDES

PEOPLE live well together when they affirm each other as separate human beings. This includes respect for our children's privacy. Privacy is a sacred key to becoming spiritual beings. Mother Teresa once said, "We need to find God, and he cannot be found in noise and restlessness. God is the friend of silence."[5] Giving our children privacy is adding a vital nutrient to the good ground of our homes.

I recently went back to some of my old neighborhoods with my parents. As we rounded the corner and drove up to the house my dad built on Cecil Avenue in Campbell, California, we could tell immediately that the owners had not maintained the house. It was shabby and in need of paint. The grass was choked with weeds and was cluttered with junk.

I was surprised by a warm feeling that invaded me as I gazed at that house, especially since it was the most run-down house we had visited that day. I stopped and pondered for a moment what this warmth was all about. I kept staring at the house, the street, and the yard. Things had changed so much in forty-five years. It was now backed up against a shopping mall, and all the surrounding lots contained houses. "Most of the lots were vacant when I built this house," my father remarked. "We were the first ones out here."

Memories began to come back. I remembered a grove of walnut trees that had stood on the adjoining lot. The trees had been removed long ago, but the memory of one tree stood out. It was a large tree with a trunk painted white. I had taken scraps of wood from the construction site while my dad was building this house and made a tree house in that tree. I had tied a large rope to a higher branch so that I could swing down for a quick exit.

Up there it had seemed that I could see forever. I had felt as if I were on top of the world. It had been my fortress. When other kids came down the street, I could spy on them without being seen.

I felt like a child again, remembering something that had belonged to me and no one else. It had been my sanctuary. There I could think, consider, ponder, dream, imagine, and talk to myself and God. I remembered feeling in touch with myself in that little tree house made of discarded scraps of wood. Standing there that day, I wondered if I had given our children good places of solitude.

Teaching our children to have a private life, to appreciate solitude, is teaching them to listen to the inner life. Bedrooms, letters, journals, and places of solitude are a part of that private life. Parents who invade this privacy, who snoop and eavesdrop, are not allowing their children to discover who they really are. Encourage your family members to be alone at times, not just as a form of time-out punishment, but as a rich luxury for finding meaning from life.

All of us need ways to hide parts of ourselves from the gawking eyes and ears of others. This includes not only places of privacy for our thoughts but privacy for our bodies as well. We all have a right to distinguish our bodies from all others and to keep them private.

One of my most painful and vivid boyhood memories was having to take class showers following physical education in junior high school. I'm not sure if anything has changed, but when I was in junior high, schools gave little thought to protecting an underdeveloped boy's privacy. I was a late bloomer, still a little boy in many ways. It seemed to me that most of the other boys were fully developed. I was the frequent subject of ridicule and teasing.

My physical-education instructor, who was also the football coach, was a macho military type. He pressed us with physical tests like climbing ropes and doing a series of push-ups and sit-ups. If we didn't measure up to his standards, he would berate us in front of the other kids. "Carmichael!" he would scream. "Even the girls can climb that rope higher than you can! What kind of a wimp are you anyway?" The boys watching and listening would find great humor in his verbal abuse, until it was their turn.

But the worst thing was the showers. The boys took one look at my physical anatomy and confirmed the coach's accusations. I felt violated. To this day I dislike taking showers in public places.

Privacy is necessary to know the deepest part of ourselves. Giving children privacy is, in a sense, like giving them clothing. By the time children reach the age of five or six, they develop a healthy sense of body privacy. Parents, especially the opposite-sex parent, should respect their privacy. This is not because we want to teach our children to be prudes but because we want them to develop a sense of their private selves. Personal privacy helps children to discover who they are. It is how they develop physical boundaries.

Have you ever observed a child carrying on a dialogue with himself or herself? Have you ever observed a child making faces in a mirror? These are outward expressions of what must go on inside if our children are to know themselves. It's like trying on clothes. The outward appearance and expression are indicative of the inner, private person.

When children have privacy, they develop a sense of personal boundaries. They learn what it means not only to have their own space but also to respect others' space.

⚘ Creating a Sense of Peace
**When the fish aren't biting,
banging on the water with an oar won't help.**
CHUCK SWINDOLL

ASK yourself these questions: Do I run my home more like a military boot camp or more like a spiritual retreat center? Are my children more often "on trial" or "on leave"? Is my parenting style more like that of a drill sergeant or a counselor? Each home has a combination of these characteristics, but the styles that seem to dominate tell us something about whether we are creating a sense of peace in our homes. There is no refuge without peace.

My dad is of Scottish descent. I was always told that the Scotch and Irish are loud and boisterous because that is the way God made them. When I visited my grandparents' home when I was a kid, I heard many lively discussions about subjects ranging from politics to the best way to make piecrust. And they were not quiet discussions. People who wanted to be heard had to interrupt and yell louder than the next person. Extended-family gatherings often sounded more like a barroom on New Year's Eve than quiet family get-togethers.

More times than I can count, I have heard my father's impassioned perspectives about the latest ills of this nation. And even now, at age eighty-four, he will become very intense about certain subjects. If someone gets him going, look out! He will tell you the facts as he knows them in a style that rivals that of any street-corner evangelist. And he expects and wants his listeners to enter in, interrupt when they feel like it, and emphasize their key points with yelling and hand waving. I thought this was a perfectly normal form of conversation— until I got married.

Nancie was raised in the house of a stoic Swedish farmer. She cannot recall ever hearing her father raise his voice even once when she was growing up. She heard no loud verbal "discussions" between her parents. Stubborn? Yes. Loud? Never. According to her, it just didn't happen.

You already know what happened when we got married. The first time I raised my voice, Nancie was not only shocked, she wondered what awful thing she had done to get me so angry. And my response, with an even louder voice, was, "GOOD GRIEF, NANCIE, I'M NOT ANGRY! WE'RE JUST HAVING A DISCUSSION!"

My children have tended to side with their mother on this issue. One of my son's favorite stories is to contrast the way his mother and father woke him each morning for school. His mom, quietly shuffling into the room with the ceiling light still off, would say in a soft, lilting voice, "Good morning, honey. Did you sleep well?" She would sit at the foot of his bed and gently rub his feet.

His dad, on the other hand, would bound up the stairs, bang open the door, flip on the lights, and yell, "HEY, BUDDY, YOU GONNA SLEEP ALL DAY OR WHAT? TIME TO GET UP. NOW!" The nurturer versus the drill sergeant.

Nancie calls my "discussion" tone of voice "screaming." I have defended myself on this issue for years, calling up all the genetic arguments I learned as a kid. But I suspect she is right. While I will probably never agree to the "screaming" definition ("SCREAMING," I argue, "IS SHRILL. AND I'M NOT SHRILL!"), I can now see that my tone of voice is often intimidating. More than once I have seen tears come to my children's eyes as I "discussed" with them an issue that had me irritated. At times my verbal assaults have caused my children to recoil and shrink back within themselves like a turtle in a shell.

While I think I have made some progress on this and I am a bit more mellow now, I still struggle with this unwelcome habit. My own mistakes have given me the chance to observe firsthand what a lack of peace can do to a child's sense of refuge. Home does not feel like a refuge if a climate of peace is not there. Arguments, sibling rivalry, bickering, ungratefulness, competitive attitudes, and what my wife calls screaming will wear down family members and erode the harmony of home.

Providing our homes with a climate of peace means that the atmosphere does not put the family members on a sense of perpetual alert. We speak in softer tones. We accuse and interrogate less. We lovingly insist that family members respect each other and that while we may disagree and confront, we do it in a way that does not diminish the other person. The ultimate goal is to build each other up. Putting the habit of peace into the good ground of our home means that our children will not feel that an attack is imminent. Self-defense mechanisms can relax a bit in a climate of peace. I offer you the advice I have given myself: *Chill out.* As a wise man once said, "A gentle answer turns away wrath, but harsh words stir up anger."[6]

✿ Fostering a Climate of Simplicity

**Look at the lilies and how they grow.
They don't work or make their clothing.**
MATTHEW 6:28

AN ESSENTIAL part of making our homes places of refuge is simplicity. The very idea of refuge speaks of an unhurried pace, an uncluttered space, a sense of order. Simplicity says, "I am who I am." I don't need to appear any wiser, sexier, younger, or richer than I really am. I don't have anything to prove. Simplicity can remove a lot of anxiety from our lives.

When I was a boy, my father had his financial ups and downs. At times the cash flow was abundant because he would sell a house he built or because he earned a large contract for a custom home. But more often we waited for a house to sell, or work was scarce. It often seemed that we lived either in feast or in famine.

I recall one Christmas when my parents were dead broke. Things had not gone well. My father had fallen off a scaffold and had broken both of his legs and an arm. He was in a virtual body cast. Since he could not work, we had no money for gifts. But that year I remember as a very special Christmas. My sister and I took jobs to help out. I recall being keenly grateful for food and shelter and simple things. Somehow the experience of that Christmas sharpened our awareness of God's provision and caring. I recall the thankfulness in all of our hearts that we were alive, together, and loved. That Christmas proved to me that simplicity itself is a treasure.

Nancie and I have had much more to give our children than our parents had. Nancie asked me recently if I remembered what I got for Christmas this past year. I could not recall any gifts but one. She had the same problem. We quizzed our children, and they also couldn't recall what they had received. This wasn't because the gifts were not nice ones but because we have so much stuff that it blends together in meaninglessness. When you have several pairs of shoes and you have the capacity and the habit of buying shoes whenever you see a pair you want, receiving new shoes has no significance.

Parents need to consider doing less. Holidays, gifts, and vacations do not have to be spectacular and extravagant to be meaningful. They can be simple and inexpensive and still carry the intended significance.

Few things are more stressful than succumbing to the lure of stuff. It is easy to get into the trap of wanting and "needing" more: bigger houses, better cars, more entertainment, newer gadgets. While some people call this the American dream, it more often turns into the American nightmare.

Think about it. Stuff imprisons us. I barely escaped the trap recently when I was tempted to buy a used motor home. I gave myself this speech: "Bill, if you buy this, you are going to have to make payments on it. You will have to insure it, and you will have to clean it and find the place to store it. Ultimately you will have to repair it, and you will feel guilty if you don't use it a lot. Time you are spending on something else now will need to be sacrificed to spend time in the motor home. Your adult kids are going to want to borrow it, and you will feel bad if you refuse and worried if you agree. Are you certain you want to obligate yourself to this thing?" I decided I didn't want that motor home after all.

When we live in simplicity, we make a statement with our lives. We are saying that God is our provider. We see life and days and sunshine as gifts. We stop trying to control and manipulate. We stop fussing and positioning. We stop striving for what perishes. We become wise enough not to chase illusions. Most of all, we start hearing God's voice again. When this happens, the magic of happiness returns.[7]

Living simply also helps us give our families a sense of order, predictability, and sameness. Rituals of dinner together, a place for everything, a routine that helps the family function, shared daily and weekly chores, and a reasonably well-planned schedule all help provide a sense of security.

It is a strange paradox, but having less can mean having more. Simplicity can sharpen the senses and make us much more aware of life. Having less stuff can mean having more thankfulness, grace, appreciation, and joy. John Burroughs, writer and naturalist, once said, "I am bound to praise the simple life, because I have lived it and found it good."[8]

On June 29, 1993, Nancie and I stood at the graveside of her mother, Harriet Pearson, who had died and was now being buried next to Nancie's father, who had died a few years earlier. Nancie's mother was a very special person. When I met Harriet, she had already experienced a hard life. With broken relationships, the untimely death of much of her immediate family, severe illness, and raising seven children on the stark plains of Montana, she would have had the right to be bitter, even cynical, with life and with God. Instead, she was a sparkler of grace and humor. She had learned to plant flowers in the desert of disappointment. She had discovered how to live with contagious joy. Out of only a few simple material goods, she had created a place of refuge for her family. In her presence I always felt at home, safe, cherished.

As we stood with a small gathering of Harriet's children, loved ones, and friends, I read aloud the words of the ancient writer who said of God: "Lord, you have been our dwelling place throughout all generations. . . . He who dwells in the shelter of the Most High will rest in the shadow of the Almighty. I will say of the Lord, 'He is my refuge and my fortress, my God, in whom I trust.' Surely he will save you from the fowler's snare and from the deadly pestilence. He will cover you with his feathers, and under his wings you will find refuge; his faithfulness will be your shield and rampart. You will not fear the terror of night, nor the arrow that flies by day . . . for he will command his angels concerning you to guard you in all your ways."[9]

To be a house of refuge means to be a place where our children are kept and held, where they feel safe. It is the harbor, the fortress, and the warm fire all in one. As I read those underlined passages from Harriet's own well-worn Bible, it occurred to me that she had been God's tangible expression of those words to her children. She had been the embodiment of the place of refuge for her children.

TILLING THE GROUND
Questions for Thought and Reflection

As you think about how you can practice the habit of making your home a place of refuge, record your thoughts in a journal or notebook. Then share your reflections with your spouse or a close friend, asking them to pray for you and help you to put into practice some of the things about which you have been convicted.

1. What was your childhood "place" like, and how does it differ from where you live now?
2. The Bible says, "God is our refuge and strength." What does that mean to you?
3. In what ways are you a safe person to live with?
4. What aspects of your person could you change to make those around you feel safer?
5. What do you do to make your children feel unconditional acceptance?
6. What do you do to threaten their sense of acceptance?
7. What can you do to help create private times and quiet times for yourself and your family?
8. Have you ever had your privacy violated? If so, how did it make you feel?
9. What is your tone of voice when you are trying to get your

children to behave or when trying to make a point? How does it affect your children?

10. In what ways is your life simple? complex? How would you like to see it change?

CHAPTER 3

Formation
Who Am I?

*Teach your children to choose the right path,
and when they are older, they will remain upon it.*

PROVERBS 22:6

🌿 Who Am I?

A sense of Deity is inscribed on every heart.

JOHN CALVIN

RECENTLY Nancie and I were guests at a fund-raising banquet. It also happened to be the national take-your-daughter-to-work day. Our waiter had brought his ten-year-old daughter, Julie, with him to work, and she was assisting him at our table. As he stood in the corner of the room and gave Julie instructions about serving the salads, a woman at our table was telling us about her work as a hospital chaplain. When Julie brought our salads, she beamed at the woman. As the girl left, the woman remarked, "That child looks familiar, but I can't place where I've seen her."

Our conversation continued, and Julie came back to remove our salad plates. Again the woman commented, "I know that girl from somewhere." As Julie and her father were serving the main course, the woman stopped the girl and said, "Honey, do I know you? You look so familiar."

Julie smiled broadly as if the woman were teasing her. "You know me!" she chided.

"I do?" questioned the woman. "How? I can't place where I have seen you. Where have we met?"

The girl, now sensing that the woman really could not place her, said, "I'm your niece!"

"Oh, my," the woman said in embarrassed tones, suddenly recognizing the child. "I didn't recognize you. You have grown so much since I saw you last!" The woman felt obligated to explain to all of us at the table that she had many nieces and this child was connected to her through her former husband.

THE WOMAN'S comments shook me. They made me wonder how Julie felt about herself when her own aunt didn't know who she was. From the time children are infants, they form their view of themselves on the basis of the people around them. They begin to receive important messages about life and about who they are. As children grow, they begin to answer these important questions: Who am I? Who are my parents? How is life to be lived? They watch, they listen, they try out behaviors. Through these observations they begin their formation of who they will become.

If parents are to create good ground in which their children's character can be formed, they must realize that they are the primary message senders about who their children are. Parents communicate powerful messages through their expressions, their gestures, their emotions, their examples, and their values.[1]

The home environment is the essential building block in helping children understand who they are. Home is where we learn that we are created in the image of God, with the ability to think, choose, feel, control our passions, and serve. In the home children learn that personhood carries with it the potential for love, virtue, commitment, work, self-discipline, hope, and, ultimately, full reconciliation with their Creator.

Housed in the repository of our ancestry are all the ingredients for grace, charity, reflection, choice, heroism, nobility,
and devotion. These are the intangibles that make us distinctly
separate from all other forms of life, that make us descendants
of almighty God. Home is the place in which our lifelong quest
for godlikeness begins. PBS film critic Michael Medved said,
"What matters ultimately in the culture wars is what we do in
our daily lives–not the big statements that we broadcast to the
world at large, but the small messages we send through our
families and our neighborhoods and our communities."[2]

By observing and participating in the family, children
begin to answer questions like "What are the most essential
things in life?" "What is success?" "What brings satisfaction?" Parents cannot avoid sending character-forming messages to their children. The question becomes, Which
messages are we sending?

- Life is a wonderful adventure.
- Life is a series of disappointments.
- The focus of life is to accumulate stuff.
- Success equals money.
- Getting an education is number one.
- God has a purpose for everyone.
- Serving others is the best way to spend our time.
- People can't be trusted.
- Being healthy is number one.
- If you want people to respect you, you need to push to
  get ahead.
- Don't let anybody push you around.
- Get what you can, even if you have to cheat or step on others.

- You are important even if you are not the best athlete or student.
- Your ideas are valuable to others.
- Pursuit of pleasure is number one.
- Knowing God is number one.
- A good marriage is worth developing.
- Doing God's will is satisfying.

Most of us send a combination of messages like these to our children. When our children finally leave the refuge of home, these learned attitudes about life will play like tape recordings in their minds. All decisions and impulses will be flavored by these early images about self, family, and the why of life.

Powerful influences at home help form our view of life: what to love and what to hate, what to embrace and what to abhor, what to value and what to disregard. Home is the workshop for learning that virtue is practiced through teamwork, discipline, commitment, cooperation, negotiation, honesty, sharing, compassion, and caring. Home is where we learn how to cope with adversity, pain, postponement of gratification, and even death. Home is where we first learn to answer that foundational question: Who am I?

✒ Mentoring Our Children

The people who influence us most
are not those who buttonhole us and talk to us,
but those who live their lives like the stars in heaven
and the lilies in the field, perfectly simply and unaffectedly.
Those are the lives that mold us.

OSWALD CHAMBERS

ONE day as our ten-year-old son, Andy, and I were driving to the grocery store after I had picked him up from school, he turned to me and spontaneously said, "Dad, I love you for your commitment." This was a bit unusual to hear out of the blue and on the way home from school. Frankly, I didn't know he even knew the meaning of the word *commitment,* and I didn't understand what had prompted this remark.

"Thank you, Andy," I replied. "But tell me more of what you mean."

"Well," he said, "I love you for your commitment to Mom and to me and to our family. Johnny Hampton's parents are getting a divorce, and I just wanted you to know I love you for your commitment."

At that moment, even though Andy did not realize it, he gave me one of the greatest compliments a son could ever give his father. He had observed my vows to my wife and family in action on a day-to-day basis, and without ever asking the specific question, he had observed that I was a man who wasn't going to abandon him or his mother. What's more, he had picked up the fact that this was a desirable virtue that should be a part of every person's character repertoire.

I wish I could say that my life always teaches our children positive character traits. Unfortunately, they have also picked up some of my less desirable characteristics. It only serves to prove the awesome power of example.

Some things, like Bible verses, songs, and stories, are taught with our *words.* Other things, like the benefit of finishing a task or postponing gratification, are taught by *experience.* Still other things, like keeping vows, faithfulness, honesty, and loyalty, are taught by *example.* It is most often the things taught by example that shape our character. People can have knowledge and even some self-discipline without possessing character, but they cannot be people of integrity without possessing character.

Someone has said, "Children need models more than they need critics." Parents, be aware that the choices you continually make—from keeping the speed limit to choosing what to watch on television to treating your crabby neighbor with patience—help to teach your children their ultimate code of character. This is the real rub for most of us. Most of the character lessons we learn as children are caught, not taught. Practicing a do-as-I-say-not-as-I-do type of teaching will not work. Children will follow what we *do* much more than what we *say*.

We parents must teach our children to value the gift of choice. Children need to know that they have the ability to control a part of their destiny, that they will continually come to crossroads where they will have to choose between right and wrong, and that choosing the right way is not only noble but also brings its own great reward. Writer Phyllis Theroux in *Night Lights* said, "Small boys learn to be large men in the presence of large men who care about small boys."[3]

It is not an easy thing to raise children of virtue because it requires that we parents forgo some pleasure and submit *ourselves* to a virtuous agenda. If we are not willing to make a personal commitment to character formation, we can forget about seeing character develop in our children. Virtue is not taught with words. Sometimes it will require us to go the extra mile, to make a sacrifice, to suffer, and to postpone gratification. It will require us to do the right thing, which often is the hard thing. While our sinful nature urges us to take the easy way out, to betray virtue, we must look to God for the courage and strength to do the right thing. Isaiah the prophet reminds us, "All of us have strayed away like sheep!"[4] It is in us to stray, to betray virtue, and it takes a miracle of redemption to do otherwise.

When your eight-year-old answers the phone and you tell him to tell the caller you are not there, you are teaching your child that lying is acceptable. These are not small things, and a dose of occasional truth or lectures about truth are not going to cut it. It is an awesome thing to know that the children at your knees are learning how to live by watching and listening to you. Whether you like it or not, you are your children's mentors. Face it: A lot of what we *are* determines what our children *will be,* and no amount of rationalization for wrong behavior can ever change that fact.

✑ Giving Our Children a Moral Education

Education does not mean teaching people what they do not know.
It means teaching them to behave as they do not behave.
JOHN RUSKIN

MORAL education begins at home. In the safety of the family, children learn about right and wrong, forgiveness and grace.

When I was seven years old, we lived in a house around the corner from Woody's Homemade Ice Cream store. On hot summer days my mother would take my sister, brother, and me to Woody's for ice cream. We would take our cones and sit on our front porch, savoring our scoops of rocky road, toasted almond, strawberry, or butter brickle, sharing licks of each others' flavors. Those were good times.

At a nickel a scoop, ice cream was a treat I could sometimes afford to buy on my own. One day I had a nickel and headed out for Woody's to get a cone. However, I had a dilemma. My brother, Jimmy, was with me, and he had no money. I pondered sharing a cone with him, but greed was working its charm on my mind. Suddenly I came up with what I thought was a creative solution. "Jimmy," I said, "wait here around the corner while I go into Woody's and buy an ice-cream cone for you." I soon returned with a scoop of rocky road and handed the cone to my delighted brother. "Don't eat any until I get back," I said. I wanted to be sure my scheme worked before I let Jimmy eat the whole cone by himself. I returned to Woody's and said to him with a sad face, "I dropped my ice-cream cone, Woody. Can I get another one?"

Woody smiled down at me and said, "Sure, Billy. Be more careful this time." He served up another scoop of rocky road.

"Thanks, Woody," I said, incredulous that it had been so easy to con Woody out of another cone. When Jimmy and I came home with chocolate on our faces and shirts, my mother began to quiz us. My five-year-old brother confessed what had happened in about ten seconds flat.

My mother's response was swift. She knew I was the ringleader, so the heat was on me. She began to tell me about the moral laws I had broken. Theft, lying, cheating, and setting a bad example for my younger brother were on the list. She marched me back to Woody's so I could confess my crime and pay him another nickel, which I had to earn back with chores. My restoration continued that evening with a confession to my father when he returned from work. I will never forget my father's words. "Character, Billy," he said, "is what you are when no one else is looking."

I learned more from that nickel-ice-cream-cone crime than all the sociology textbooks could ever have taught because my parents were intent on giving me a moral education. I knew that what I did was wrong. This was not just the cute and clever antic of a seven-year-old. In our family this was a serious breach of a character quality called integrity.

Many studies show that when people can cheat, they will. If a store clerk gives people too much change, most people today will keep it. Cheating on income tax, submitting fraudulent insurance claims, shoplifting, stealing office supplies, cheating on exams, cheating on a spouse, lying on resumes to get the job, inflating government work bids, writing bad checks, using people for personal gain, and a host of other wrong behaviors are common. Having integrity seems to be a forgotten virtue for many people.

Virtues like honesty and integrity begin in the formative years while children are under the influence of their parents. Could it be that these virtues are in short supply in some families because we have devalued the idea that we are created in the image of God? A popular idea about Homo sapiens is that we are nothing more than an extension of the animal kingdom. Young adults who are now parenting children were taught this in school. What's more, they were also taught that we are a species with unalienable rights to uninterrupted pleasure (*pleasure* being the contemporary definition of what our Constitution terms *happiness*). In this system, personal gratification becomes the utmost achievement in life. We live life for pleasure, and our number one goal becomes seeking, finding, and experiencing that pleasure.

Young parents who subscribe to this view avoid most things that would require sacrifice, postponement of gratification, pain, or confrontation. And they certainly don't want to face up to any consequences of self-indulgent behaviors. In this environment, life becomes what we can get, not what we can give. Greed, selfishness, and vice take over. We become the ultimate Me. Human life becomes utilitarian.

One of our favorite family vacations is our annual fishing trip to Canada's pristine ocean waters on the inner side of Vancouver Island. Every night after fishing for halibut and salmon, we return to the little fishing village of Port Hardy. The tides run big in the Queen Charlotte straits. At times the deep ocean waters run like a river through the narrow passages between timber-covered, mountainous islands. In fact, "the drift," as we call it, can take a boat a long way from the port. An eight-knot tide in a low-lying fog can throw off a boat's direction dramatically. Even experienced seagoers can wind up miles from the entrance to the port when they miscalculate the drift. Our boat has drifted more than once, and when the fog lifted, I have looked around for the port and wondered, "How did we wind up here?"

I find this same principle true in my own and my family's values. If I am not careful to compute the drift, life can take me a long way from where I want to be. I confess that I have been there. The pursuit of a business deal, the amenities of the good life, and approval from others have thrown me off course at times. It is not that my intentions were wrong.

I planned to make the port. I thought I set my compass on the right heading. I just got caught up in a fast tide. The drift caught me by surprise.

Parents need to be vigilant so that their families do not drift. The rising tide of popular culture can take us a long way from where we intend to be if we do not consciously pay attention to where we are headed. Popular thought would have us believe that we can launch into the sea of life without a compass. Who cares about navigation if there is no destination? Many people accept the idea that God changed his moral code around 1963. Today anything goes. And if we are not careful, when our eighteen-year-olds walk out the door and into adult life, we will be asking ourselves, "How did we wind up here?"

Embracing relative values rather than absolute values is like placing our children in a boat on the sea, without a compass, without landmarks, without teaching them how to read the stars, and without any knowledge of which way is north, east, south, or west. They become lost. They have no idea where they came from, where they are going, how to get there, or even why they should go.

Families become lost when they have no vision of the way things ought to be. As a nation, we become increasingly divided when we do not have a shared vision of right and wrong, good and bad, holy and unholy, sacred and secular. This is not new. Thousands of years ago, a wise man said, "Where there is no vision, the people perish."[5]

Some people would argue that there are problems with any shared vision, including the Judeo-Christian one. Christians have historically allowed such things as slavery and racial discrimination to flourish in this country. I would agree. I do not excuse the sins we commit. Our nation is like a house we share as living quarters. There's a lot of dirt and clutter still left in this house—things like prejudice, injustice, dishonesty, greed, and lust. There is no doubt that we need to clean our house.

But taking away the shared vision of the way things ought to be is like burning down the house. If we have no house to share as living space (i.e., a set of values we agree are right and other behaviors we agree are wrong), we have no way of working together to clean it up. If we do not value the same house or living space, we become distant neighbors and eventually reclusive enemies.

When we define values as "mine" or "yours," we destroy the notion of absolute values. The contemporary code of "doing good" translates "You don't call me into question, and I won't call you into question." "Love your neighbor as yourself" is translated to mean "Leave your neighbors alone, and they will do the same for you." "I want to do it, so I will" is the contemporary attitude. If we are to build healthy homes, we must resist these trends by setting godly examples and discussing with our children the flaws in this thinking.

In his book *The De-Valuing of America,* former Secretary of Education Bill Bennett wrote, "Nature abhors a vacuum; so does a child's soul. If that soul is not filled with noble sentiments, with virtue, if we do not attend to the 'better angels of our nature,' it will be filled by something else."[6] Today's children need to be taught that the gift of choice carries with it an awesome responsibility. This gift was not given to any other form of life on earth, and it is the beginning of what makes us different from the rest of the animal kingdom. Choice is the door to our spirit, and it is our spirit nature that is the part of us created in God's image.

Children also need to be shown by example that moral choices comes in two types: right ones and wrong ones. Right choices fall in line with the patterns of godly behavior. It's important to teach our children that submitting our right to choose to the higher good of choosing what is ethical and moral is a noble and spiritual act. Our children need to experience the fact that sometimes choosing to suffer is the right choice. Our children need to be taught that even dying for their principles is better than selling their souls for a season of pleasure.

The idea of resisting temptation and refraining from indulgence is disappearing from the cultural landscape of many homes. Professor Allan Bloom in *The Closing of the American Mind* said, "We are like ignorant shepherds living on a site where great civilizations once flourished. The shepherds play with the fragments that pop up to the surface, having no notion of the beautiful structures of which they were once a part."[7] Moral codes of behavior, taught and embraced for thousands of years, are there to help families in their struggle to raise godly children.

When principles of character become a part of our moral fabric, they serve as guidelines about how to act and what to do. Most of us can reflect and say, "I should have done this or that," but genuine character development will give us the tools and principles to make the right choices *at the time* action is needed. Prisons are filled with people who look back and know they made a mistake, but their lack of character at the moment of committing the crime kept them from acting on what was right.

Most parents say they value character, that they want their children to be men and women with moral convictions. I am sure you do too. But do your children know what moral character looks like? I sometimes cringe when my children describe some of the people they admire—sports heroes who batter their wives, or Hollywood notables who reflect immoral and violent characters not only in the parts they play but also in real life. It is easy for children to mistake performance for character if we parents don't point this out and point our children to other more noble heroes. If we laud people who entertain us but who lack moral character, we teach our children that the things we really cherish have nothing at all to do with virtue.

As parents we must teach our children that qualities like morality and integrity do not always give immediate reward. As pastor and author Douglas Rumford said, "Full grown oaks are not produced in three years; neither are servants of God."[8] We often see those who cheat prospering for a time. That is why the pursuit of character must be its own reward. Our children need to see from our example that to resist the animal drive toward self-pleasure, to endure the pain of self-denial, to postpone gratification, to buck the tide of popular opinion, to hold to principles of character, and to reject some popular behaviors simply because they are wrong is the highest form of happiness.

Henry Van Dyke said, "It is only by thinking about great and good things that we come to love them, and it is only by loving them that we come to long for them, and it is only by longing for them that we are impelled to seek after them; and it is only by seeking after them that they become ours."[9]

For people created in the image of God, indulging in unending pleasure is not enough. We value a good name, trust, honesty, hard work, accountability, self-denial, sacrifice, charity, moral goodness, and even laying down our lives for the principles we believe.[10] We call it *character,* and it is time to restore it to its rightful place of esteem in the human spirit and in our homes. It is clearly the stuff of good ground.

And what does character development bring us and our children? First, it can bring true happiness as individuals. Second, it can bring order and peace to our society and stability to our families. Third, it can bring caring and compassionate solutions to the problems we face on earth. And finally, it can bring us closer to a right relationship with God.

❧ Guarding Our Expectations

When parents' desires and dreams for their child get in the way of the child's own hopes, I find the blueprint for disaster.
KIRBY HANAWALT

IT IS easy to confuse our goals for our children's character formation with our personal expectations of them. This happens when we parents have strong ideas and ambitions for our children. It is not wrong to want the best for our children and to encourage them to do their best, but we must guard against the tendency to let *our* expectations get in the way of their God-given gifts.

My friend David is a successful medical doctor with a growing practice in specialized medicine. Recently he told me a story about his childhood. Dave's father was born into a peasant family in Eastern Europe. When Dave's father was still a boy, the family immigrated to America. This family had no education and was accustomed to hard manual labor. When Dave's father was eleven years old, his parents made him quit school and get a job as an errand boy to help support the family. All of the family's six siblings helped in this way. "My grandfather felt that people should work, and the message he gave to my father was that education was not work," Dave said.

But in his heart, Dave's father yearned to get an education. Dave describes him as a highly motivated man. Eventually the father went back to school and graduated from high school at the age of twenty-three. By the time he was twenty-nine, he had earned his Ph.D. in biochemistry and eventually became a leading research scientist.

Dave's father had a dream that someday his son would become a doctor. Dave said his father often told him, "You can do anything you put your mind to." From an early age, Dave knew that his father wanted him to become a doctor.

"It wasn't so much what my father said to me," said Dave. "It was simply that to my father, science was the pinnacle of worthy pursuits. Anything less was a step down. It was very subtle. He never said, 'You will go to medical school.' It was just an unspoken assumption for as long as I can remember."

Dave says he remembers when he learned that he had not been accepted to a local medical school to which he had applied. "I came back to the car where my father was, and fainted. I literally passed out. My father, a very gentle and loving man—but very determined—said, 'That's okay, Son, we'll just apply somewhere else.'"

Dave's father made some contacts and got him admitted
to another medical school. At first Dave was not getting adequate grades. "The stress was incredible," he said. In fear of
disappointing his father, he studied almost day and night.
Driven to work harder, Dave began to succeed. By the time he
was a third-year student in medical school, Dave was at the
top of his class. He was elected to a prestigious fraternity containing only the top twelve medical students.

Dave telephoned his father to let him know of his achievement, and in the course of conversation, his father said,
"Now you are in a good position to go on and get a Ph.D.
also!" Dave's heart sank. He saw this as one more hurdle to
leap to keep pace with his father's expectations.

"When I was a boy, my father always had time for me. I
felt unconditional love from my father," said Dave. "But at the
same time, I felt tremendous pressure to fulfill his expectations. I never felt his love for me was contingent on my success, but I felt that I would disappoint him if I didn't live up to
his dreams for me."

Dave confessed that while being a medical doctor has
allowed him to experience success, he continues to have
nagging doubts about whether it has been the best use of
his natural gifts. "In a way, I feel trapped by what I am doing.
I feel I'm living the career that my parents chose for me," he
said. Dave resents the fact that he never had any other
options. "It's as if I never got to see the menu," he said. "I
feel that my parents ordered for me."

One of the most compelling urges we have as parents is
to see our children prosper. Every generation dreams that its
children will succeed to a greater degree than it did. While

this is a natural desire, it can become obsessive and a huge source of stress to our children.

In their book *Family Fears,* Jack and Jerry Schreur point to research that indicates that of the top five "family fears," number two is "the fear that our children will not turn out right," followed only by the fear that "our children will make life-dominating mistakes."[11] Couple these two fears, and you can have a powerful motivation to drive the expectations for your children to the limit. In *Hide or Seek,* psychologist Dr. James Dobson writes, "The vast majority of our children are not dazzlingly brilliant, extremely witty, highly coordinated, tremendously talented, or universally popular! They are just plain kids with oversized needs to be loved and accepted as they are."[12]

Unfortunately for many children, their success is determined by their parents' selfish expectations. If our children fail to reach the goals we set for them, we feel like failures. In other words, we parents feel that our children will reflect negatively on us.

It helps me to remember that my children are not extensions of me. When we live vicariously through our children, we are meeting *our* needs, not theirs. Pushing our children to excel in our dreams or admonishing them to be more macho or more feminine can be very damaging to their development and sense of security. Children are vessels to be molded in a highly individual way. God is shaping them with their own unique gifts and personalities. They are not like trophies in a display case.

In a recent visit to the East Coast, I listened to one of my colleagues speak with disappointment about his son who graduated from college, floundered around for a while, and then went to Africa to work with poor people. His son was living with poor families, eating their food, and sleeping in their huts. He was learning their language and trying to give them help where he could. The father saw this as a disappointing failure, as if his son had given up all his dreams of a better life.

The irony was that while this father spoke in tones of failure because it was not the fulfillment of *his* expectations for his son, I was thinking how wonderful I would feel if this were one of my sons. Early on I had hoped one of our children would become a missionary. At the time of our conversation, my oldest son, who was about the same age as my friend's son, was the research coordinator for the heart-transplant unit of a major medical university. "You must be very proud," my friend said wistfully. Yes, I *was* proud of my son, but his comments made me aware of how powerful our expectations of our children are and how they tend to shape how we view them.

The son of this man has since returned from Africa. He has studied French and Portuguese, speaks fluent Swahili, and has been accepted into a prestigious engineering school. His goal is still to help developing Third World countries, but now his father speaks in glowing terms of his son's achievements because he "fits" the father's expectations of him.

One of the ways we impose expectations on our children early on is through competition with other children. This can happen in any venue, such as grades or music, but it is especially true in athletics. Many parents today are vicariously living out their own unfulfilled dreams by investing themselves in a commitment to see their children excel in some competitive sport.

When I was a child, we played games. I remember going outside with a ball and bat and finding a few neighborhood kids to play with. We made up rules to fit the size of the "field" in our yard and the ability of the kids available. We also played games like kick the can. We organized the games ourselves, made up our own rules through negotiation, and played by our own timetable.

Today children rarely have time for this kind of noncompetitive play. Organized sports accept children at such an early age that they are barely walking before their parents have them enrolled for lessons and competition. We dress five- and six-year-olds in uniforms and put them under experienced and "motivated" coaches who can teach them how to win. We buy them expensive lessons at the local ice-skating rink or dance school.

Messages that transmit our expectations can be very subtle but very real. Thus, playing a sport or practicing the piano when accompanied by parents' expectations can have negative consequences for both parent and child. Even when the child likes the activity, the pressure to be better or be the best can put tremendous stress, not only on the child, but on the parent-child relationship as well.

While we should not hesitate to encourage our children to do the very best they can and to put forth good effort in achieving excellence, we must constantly be examining our motives for doing so. If our intent is to help our children reach their God-given potential, then our expectations can be good. But if our intent is to make us look good or meet our own needs, then our expectations can be harmful.

Sometimes the reverse is true too. Some parents have no

expectations or even negative expectations of their children. When a parent projects that a daughter will simply grow up and have babies, with no other achievements in life, it may become a self-fulfilling prophecy. When children are told they're just like their father and won't amount to anything, that is often what will happen. When we have no expectations, we fail to give children hope and optimism. We rob our children of possibility.

Not all expectations are bad. Having healthy expectations for our children is vital to character formation. Healthy expectations would be such things as the desire that our children develop self-discipline, integrity, and a sense of justice, that they find and develop their God-given gifts, that they learn to provide for themselves and their family, and that they develop spiritually.

Parents should encourage their children to get involved in something that will teach them self-discipline, teamwork, and the rewards of hard work. Parents need to engage their children in all kinds of chores, activities, and events that will stimulate them and create family interaction as well as develop character. But as we encourage our children in these activities, we must allow for their own personality and gifts to emerge. Most of all, we need to let them know that we love them no matter what their level of ability or achievement.

Sometimes children feel smothered in their parents' success. If you are a successful high achiever, your children may get buried under your accomplishments or feel they can never achieve what you have achieved. Winston Churchill's son once said, "When you are living under the shadow of a great oak tree, the small sapling, so close to the parent tree, does not perhaps receive enough sunshine."

Children who feel the responsibility to fulfill the dreams of their parents will eventually feel cramped by this unhealthy expectation and may rebel. Guard your expectations carefully. Have expectations, dream dreams, but guard them. Make sure they are healthy expectations. And be the number one cheerleader of your children as you see them begin to develop expectations for themselves.

✒ Formation through Work

Children very often are brought up believing
they are guests in the home
because they have nothing to do except live there.
G. BOWDEN HUNT

WE ASSIST our children's character formation through how we handle work in our homes. There is something very gratifying about work. Part of creating good ground for our children is giving them responsibilities that will shape them. To rob our children of the privilege of work is to take from them a rich blessing they can experience for all of life. Remember that the highest reward for our toil is not what we *get* for it but rather what we *become* through it. Daily chores, schoolwork, homework, and teamwork are all a vital part of your children's formation. While you may pay them an allowance for their household work, remember that your children are not doing these things just for an allowance. Your children do these things because they need to be done and your children need to do them.[13]

In the spring of 1952, when I was nine years old, I wanted a new baseball glove in the worst way. Christmas and my birthday had both passed, and I needed the glove for Little League practice. My father said that he needed a helper to put up a concrete-block retaining wall at a house he was building and that if I wanted to, I could work with him to earn some money, possibly enough to buy the baseball glove.

The retaining wall was at the foot of a small hill. My father was down below laying the concrete block, and I was up on top with the mixer. "Two sand, two gravel, one lime, and one cement," I repeated to myself as I shoveled it all into an old mixer and added a measured amount of water. Then I dumped the mix down a homemade wooden chute to my father. It took us two days to build the wall, and when it was finished, my father took me to the sporting-goods store, where I picked out a most beautiful baseball glove. That experience was a formative one for me. I learned not only that work empowered me to earn the resources I needed but also that a job well done has its own internal reward. I kept that glove for many years, even after I was married, as a reminder that if I put my mind to something, I could accomplish the task and reach my goal. Work helps in our formation process because it helps to define who we are. It also gives vital experience in the formation of our children's character by requiring them to stick to a task, take responsibility, be accountable, and make an effort to do their best.

These are lessons of formation I have tried to pass on to my children. I am thankful for living in a part of the country where it snows in the winter. I am thankful that we have a woodstove to help heat our house. I am thankful that we can go out in the forest with a permit and cut our firewood. And I am thankful that I gave my four sons the privilege of cutting, hauling, splitting, and stacking countless cords of wood while they were growing up. Mind you, they did not view this chore as a privilege at the time, and they were not exactly thankful for the opportunity. But the work disciplines they were required to practice while they were growing up are paying dividends in their adult lives. Tackling a tough job, sticking to a task, following through, and finishing a project are some of the disciplines children rely on to help them through life later on.

Work is also a spiritual exercise. It is an important part of the formation of our character. When we are called to do the work we do, we find great fulfillment in the doing. Whether we serve as bus drivers or rocket scientists, doctors or ditchdiggers, we can find meaning, joy, and purpose from our work if we see it as an expression of life and God's calling for us.[14]

Most young people today think that the primary goal of work is money. It is sad if we think of occupation only as a job that gives us a paycheck so that we can enjoy the weekend. It is much deeper than that. The work that we do should be part of our calling, our response to God's leading in our lives.

When children are young, they will try on many things. "I want to be a fireman!" or "I want to be an astronaut." This trying on of various occupations is a healthy thing. It means that children are, in their own simple ways, beginning to search for their calling in life. This business goes on for some time, often not discovered for many years after they become young adults.

It is important that parents support their children in this finding process. It is unrealistic to expect our children to find what they are called to do at an early age. Deciding on a college

major is easy for some who have sensed a calling since childhood. But for most of us it is a shot in the dark. I majored in
counseling and became a publisher. A friend of mine majored in
aeronautical engineering and ended up as a successful pastor of
a large church. Matching our gifts and dreams with a hands-on
vocation is not easy. We flounder for a time trying to find it. And
it can change more than once during our lifetime. The important
thing is that our work is meaningful and that early on we learn
that doing a good job, no matter what the work, carries its own
reward. The important thing for parents to remember is that by
assigning work to our children early in life and requiring their
contribution to doing the tasks at home, we prepare them for
their future experiences with work.

The early Christians saw work as an essential virtue. The
apostle Paul said, "You know that these hands of mine have
worked to pay my own way, and I have even supplied the needs
of those who were with me. And I have been a constant example of how you can help the poor by working hard."[15]

The opposite of work is not play; it is idleness. To have
the ability and giftedness to do a necessary thing and not to
do it is to ignore God's calling. In a sense, we could say that
work is a continuation of creation. When we work, we are
extending what God wanted done, and by doing so we are
cocreators with God.[16] As Joan Chittister, a Benedictine sister, said, "In Benedictine spirituality, work is purposeful and
perfecting and valuable. It is not a time-filler or a money-
maker or a necessary evil. We work because the world is unfin-
ished, and it is ours to develop. We work with a vision in
mind. . . . Work is a commitment to God's service."[17]

Responsibility is the twin sister of work. Responsibility

comes from the word *respond,* which means "to answer." So to be answerable means to be accountable. By teaching our children to be accountable for their actions, we are instilling a sense of responsibility that will serve them well in the years ahead. As Aristotle was among the first to insist, we *become* what we are as persons by the decisions that we ourselves make.[18]

Taking responsibility not only puts the consequence of failure squarely where it belongs, it also gives us the moral and mental fortitude to work at solving our problems. This is maturity. It is immature to blame; it is mature to seek solutions. Certainly some events and circumstances are beyond our power; we didn't create them, and we can't control them. But even in these times, responsible people will seek ways to contribute to the solution. There is danger in insulating our children from work and responsibility. These disciplines are among the most important if we want our children to find the ability as adults to be accountable, to stick to a task, and to know the joy of accomplishment.

Farmers and gardeners know it takes lots of work to prepare the ground for spring planting. It also takes lots of hard work to provide good ground in which our children can grow in their ability to do and appreciate work.

Formation through Creativity

Can you imagine a group of bankers sitting around a table
when a young earnest man looks them in the eyes and says,
"I'm going to build a billion-dollar empire
based on a mouse, a fairy, and seven dwarfs. Will you help me?"
He would have been laughed out of the building.
LAURIE BETH JONES

GOD gives unique gifts to all of us. Using our creativity
to discover our gifts is an important part of character formation. It is through the lens of creativity—imagination, dreams,
games, discovery, and wonder—that children begin to see the
possibilities for their lives, helping them to form their own
character and role in the world.

Andy, our youngest son, had a unique ability to entertain
himself. When he was about four or five years old, *Star Wars*
was very popular. Through gifts from parents, siblings, aunts,
and grandparents at birthdays and Christmas, Andy had one
of the most impressive collections of *Star Wars* action figures
of anyone in our neighborhood. He also had an abundance of
plastic army figures, cowboys, and Indians. He would play for
hours, humming the *Star Wars* theme song, calling out orders
to his favorite characters, making sounds of gunfire and explo-
sions, and cheering for whichever hero was to win the game
happening in his imagination. Even now, Andy's imagination
and sense of humor never stop working. He continues to
amuse himself and all those who come in contact with him.

Andy's older brother Chris, on the other hand, let his
imagination roam through his collection of Choose Your Own
Adventure books. These books allowed him to choose a page
and determine the outcome of a story. Later Chris began to
create his own stories. Today he is a creative writer with a college degree in English. At age twenty-two, he already has successfully written and published works for children.

Our daughter, Amy, is an artist. She loves to paint and
draw, sometimes by the hour. Drawings of animals are her
favorite subjects, and I marvel at the creative ability God has
given her to work with her hands.

In his book *Quest for Character,* pastor and writer Charles Swindoll said, "Give the dreamers room. Go easy on the 'shouldn'ts' and 'can'ts,' OK? Dreams are fragile things that have a hard time emerging in a cloud of negativism."[19] All children have inside them creative sparks, and in the formative years, it is important for parents to help children discover these gifts. We help our children in their character formation by encouraging a sense of awe and wonder, by letting them daydream, and by stimulating their imaginations with stories and activities. Reading to your children from a variety of sources will help them develop their creativity. Abraham Joshua Heschel in *The Wisdom of Heschel* says, "Awe enables us to perceive in the world intimations of the divine, to sense in small things the beginning of infinite significance, to sense the ultimate in the common and the simple; to feel in the rush of the passing the stillness of the eternal."[20]

Creativity is important because it is part of the very nature of God. He is the ultimate Creator. His works are so vast and awesome that even to begin to relate to him and his creation requires us to enter into an attitude of childlike faith and wonder. Roots of hope, understanding, and invention are all found in our creativity. Creative processes help us fit life together in meaningful patterns and create new patterns that may not have been thought of before. Fixing meals and fitting together the pieces of space shuttles require a sense of creativity. Children need to discover early that they possess a treasure of imaginations that are uniquely theirs. They need to learn that by tapping into this vast resource, they can make wonderful contributions to their own life and those around them.

🌿 Formation through Hospitality

Hospitality is the way we turn a prejudiced world around, one heart at a time.

JOAN D. CHRITTISTER

THE KIDS and I love to hear Nancie tell this story:

It was Christmas Eve, 1958. Nancie's father had taken the children to town to do some last-minute Christmas shopping and run some other errands. Nancie's mother had given Gunder an extralong list of errands to run, mainly because she needed the time without kids underfoot to prepare the house for that evening's planned celebration.

Evening came in the near-blizzard conditions of northern Montana, and darkness descended. Harriet started to worry about her family. The roads looked icy, and the swirling snow made visibility difficult. The wind made mournful violin sounds as it howled around the corners of the old farmhouse. But inside—*inside*—all was warmth, candlelight, and perfection. Harriet stood back and surveyed her hard work with satisfaction. Everything shone. The house was in order, the table set with the good china, a tinsel-covered tree standing in one corner, presents wrapped and ready.

The traditional oyster stew simmered in a big kettle on the stove, and the fragrant homemade rolls stayed warm under a towel. On a stately platter stood Nancie's grandmother's traditional plum pudding with its special lemon sauce. That would be enjoyed after "the tree." Everything was perfect.

That's when someone knocked at the back door. Harriet opened it to a strange sight. At first she couldn't tell who it was standing there in a mask of snow and ice. "Oh, it's Robert!" Harriet finally recognized the man.

Robert Norton lived in a shack about five miles down the road. Folks in the community called him "Snortin' Norton" due to a never-repaired cleft palate that made talking and controlling his saliva difficult. Neighbors said that Snortin' Norton "wasn't all there mentally." It wasn't that people were intentionally mean to Robert. They did some charitable things for him. But their charity did not always include acceptance.

Now Snortin' Norton stood at the Pearsons' back door, saliva and mucus frozen, so covered by snow and ice that he was nearly unrecognizable. Harriet brought Robert in and immediately ran to get warm washcloths and towels. She gently cleaned his face. His boots left muddy puddles all over the freshly waxed floor. He mumbled that his car had careened off the road a mile away. He'd walked, searching for help to dig it out of the mounding snow.

"Of course," Harriet assured him. "The family will be home soon, and Gunder and the boys will help you. But let's get you out of those wet things."

It was then that she noticed Robert staring around the room with delight. "Oh, Robert," she said. "It's Christmas Eve! Would you like some warm stew?"

His eyes lit up. "Sure!"

Harriet reached for an everyday mug near the stove. Suddenly she stopped and hung it back on the rack. A sense of the holy came over her. *No. This was not just Snortin' Norton, poor unfortunate, retarded neighbor. The Lord himself was here . . . the King.* Harriet set a place for Robert at the table, using the best china and silver.

WHEN Nancie tells that story, she calls it "The Christmas That Jesus Paid a Visit to the Pearson Home." It was a formative event for Nancie and her siblings because the true spirit of hospitality was enfleshed in their home. As Nancie shares that story with other people, she realizes that one event that carried a powerful message and formed a caring spirit in her child-heart has carried forward and has blessed many others in the years since.

Hospitality is the ultimate form of giving to others because through it we give the greatest gift, the gift of ourselves. Hospitality originated with God. He invites us into his presence, into his kingdom. When we take people in—into our home, into our intimate circle of family, and into our hearts—we are saying to them that they matter. Hospitality is relationship. Hospitality is healing. Hospitality is the soul's embrace of others. Human beings are the only creatures on this earth capable of expressing hospitality. Showing hospitality forms our children's ideas and emotions about serving and caring for others.

Start by being hospitable with your own children and other members of your family. Practice serving each other. Let your children see you caring for your spouse's needs. Help your children take care of each other when they are sick or deeply discouraged.

After we have practiced hospitality in our own families, we can begin to reach out to others. Hospitality begins when we share something that other human beings want or need—the need to be taken in; the need to be listened to; the need to be accepted and welcomed; the need for love, food, shelter, and warmth; the need to be in fellowship and community. Hospitality is a way to nurture those outside our family and allow our children to see this virtue in action. With our eyes, expressions, and words, we not only warmly greet those invited to our door but also show our concern and interest in their lives. Questions help show we are interested in our guests' lives: How are you doing today? How is your family, your job, your physical well-being? How may I serve you?

Hospitality says, "Let me minister to you this hour. Let me give you food and shelter and my undivided attention." Hospitality is the holy act giving of ourselves wholly. Hospitality is making our guests feel celebrated.

Hospitality is a virtue that children will learn only by experience. Like so many virtues, it is caught, not taught. Writer Girt S. Disney gives a wonderful narration about hospitality in his interpretation of the gospel story about Jesus' miracle of feeding five thousand with the loaves and fishes. "I imagine that when they first began to divide five loaves and two fish among thousands of people, the disciples gave little tiny pieces. They tried to make the food go as far as it would. But as their supply did not diminish, I envision their giving away larger and larger pieces. They fairly tossed huge hunks of bread, great slices of fish. What began as a hesitant division in anticipation of want ended with an expansive excess of food for all. This was no grim religious business. Jesus played host to a feast in the desert. And I feel sure it was an hour filled with celebrative delight."[21]

Like Jesus' disciples, our children will learn from us the great joy and celebration of generous hospitality. And if our children are to grow up to be adults who care about others, we must teach them the social virtue of hospitality. For children, eye contact, politeness, and helping to prepare and serve meals is a recital for the future in the basics of hospitable behavior.

OUR HOMES are the ground in which the character of our children grows silently, lovingly, and faithfully. It is up to us to till the ground, water it, and feed it so that our children will have everything they need to become men and women of character and virtue.

TILLING THE GROUND
Questions for Thought and Reflection

As you think about how you can practice the habit of making your home a place of formation, record your thoughts in a journal or notebook. Then share your reflections with your spouse or a close friend, asking them to pray for you and help you to put into practice some of the things about which you have been convicted.

1. What messages about life and living are you sending to those around you, especially your children?
2. Do you have a good sense about who you really are? Is the real you the same person those outside the family see?
3. Who were and are your mentors? What effect have they had on you?
4. How can you be an effective mentor to your children now? In what specific areas do you want to mentor your children?
5. What do you consider to be essential aspects of giving a child a moral education? What specific things do you do to give your child a moral education?

6. Do you feel there is an absolute set of God-given values by which everyone should live? What are those absolute values? How do you teach these to your children?

7. What are your spoken and unspoken expectations for your children? In what ways are these expectations healthy or unhealthy?

8. What parts of your work do you enjoy the most and like the least? Do you do any type of charitable or volunteer work? How can you involve your children in volunteer work with you?

9. How can you make the sharing of household chores an opportunity for your children to learn responsibility and the joy of work well done?

10. How do you encourage creativity in your family?

11. How does your family demonstrate hospitality? How can you involve your children in giving hospitality?

CHAPTER 4

Boundaries
What Are the Rules?

Rules belong to life the way the scale belongs to music,
and the way grammar belongs to writing.
We cannot live the moral life without rules
anymore than we can make music without scales.
Or write a story without grammar.

LEWIS SMEDES

🌿 Setting Up Parameters

Any confusion of responsibility and ownership in our lives is a problem of boundaries.

HENRY CLOUD AND JOHN TOWNSEND

JUST as landowners fence in their property to identify its parameters, we must identify the parameters of our lives. A fenced-in yard accomplishes several things: It provides a clear limit to a child's wandering; it provides a line of protection; and it still gives some freedom for the child to explore and roam. Children need behavioral boundaries if they are to develop healthy patterns of self-discipline and accountability.

When our children are young, we establish clearly defined physical limits. It starts with a playpen and eventually expands to a fenced-in backyard. Later the boundaries become specified areas in the neighborhood. Just as these tangible parameters set physical limits, intangible boundaries help set spiritual and emotional limits. The boundaries discussed in this chapter suggest ways for you to construct a fence around the good ground of your home.

Boundaries are those intangible things that help distinguish you from someone else and that help you determine how to conduct life. Children without boundaries tend to become confused about who they are as individuals. In their book *Boundaries,* counselors Henry Cloud and John Townsend write, "Boundaries define us. They define what is me and what is not me. A boundary shows me where I end and someone else begins, leading me to a sense of ownership."[1] Cloud and Townsend go on to give us some examples of personal boundaries. *Skin* is a most basic boundary that defines an individual. We use the expression "He or she gets under my skin" to describe our feeling when someone violates our personal space or makes us uncomfortable. Our physical self is the primary way we learn to distinguish ourselves from others. It is the beginning of knowing boundaries. Victims of physical and sexual abuse often have problems with boundaries.

Words are another boundary. We can create invisible fences with our words. *No* is a basic boundary word. Words also help define our boundaries when we describe how we feel, what we like and do not like. Words describe rules, laws, and agreements that create specific boundaries.

Truth is another aspect of defining boundaries. God uses truth to describe his boundaries. When we tell the truth to others and know the truth about ourselves, it helps us define our boundaries.

Consequences are another important reality about boundaries. When we trespass another's property in the physical realm, we face consequences. We also face consequences when we trespass in the spiritual and emotional realms. God sets consequences for certain behaviors: If you obey my commandments, you will live long. Nature has consequences: If you play in the snow without proper clothing, you can get frostbite. Society has consequences for breaking the laws: If you don't stop at the stop sign, you can get a ticket and pay a fine. Parents set consequences for their children: "If you don't finish your homework, you can't go out to play."[2]

If children know where the family's boundaries begin and end, they will have a healthy sense of self and can develop healthy freedom. On the other hand, if they do not know where the boundaries are, they will be constantly searching for some definition.

One woman said to me, "I grew up in a family without limits. My dad's life revolved around his business. My mom's life revolved around Dad. My siblings and I were left to do as we pleased. When Mom did try to set a limit, I would say to her, 'Why bother telling me no? You know I'll just do it anyway.' She would only say to me, 'You're right.' I hated that! I wanted her to set and enforce the limits. As a result, I grew up feeling out of control. At age twenty-three, when I became a Christian and discovered rules and boundaries, I found security and, ironically, freedom. I still struggle setting boundaries for my kids, but I try because I want them to know love."

Clearly we all need boundaries in our lives. They are the framework on which everything else is hung. They are the lines that provide form and context. Boundaries help to define the parameters of our soul. They help me stay in touch with the real "me." By having clear boundaries, our children learn what the rules are—that yes means yes and no means no. Even more important, the boundaries we set become a vital reference point for our children when they begin to set up self-imposed boundaries as young adults.

If you think about it, most things in life have some shape,

some form and context. Can you think of one athletic game without rules and boundaries? Baseball has strikes, outs, innings, bases, and a foul-ball line. Without these, it wouldn't be baseball. Music has notes, scales, keys, and chords. It isn't music unless one stays inside these boundaries.

It is absurd to think that we can successfully raise our children without boundaries. A family without boundaries is like baseball without the rules. A family without clearly defined parameters, rules of conduct, and a sense of order will produce children who feel insecure. They will act as if they are in a sort of free fall. Family psychologist Ron Taffel calls setting up good boundaries a way of "feeling the envelope."[3] When we have set good boundaries, our children feel the envelope and will feel safe and kept.

Mental, physical, emotional, and spiritual boundaries are the keys to helping us know how to take responsibility, how to reject those things we should avoid, how to embrace those things we should follow after, and how to order our lives. When children do not have adequate boundaries, when they do not know the rules, when they are accustomed to living unordered lives, they lack the focus to become men and women of character. This is because children will find it difficult to develop inner discipline if outer discipline is lacking during their developing years.

Boundaries are not just ways to keep order in the family; they are not just methods of discipline, although they serve this purpose while our children are in our care. Healthy boundaries are more: They are an important nutrient in the good ground of your home. Without them, our children's development will be hindered. Family experts tell us that many clinical psychological symptoms, such as depression, anxiety disorders, eating disorders, addictions, impulsive disorders, guilt problems, shame issues, panic disorders, and marital and relational struggles find their root in conflicts with boundaries.[4]

It is vital for us as parents to set good parameters, good boundaries for our children. Conflicts arise when we do not know our own boundaries or we do not have good personal limits. Lack of self-discipline, frequent inability to finish a task, difficulty in confronting others in a loving way, finding it difficult to say no to those who would violate our boundaries, and issues of self-esteem are some of the symptoms evident when we have not developed good boundaries of our own.

Parents who see these tendencies in their own lives will find it more difficult to set good parameters and boundaries for their children. Parents will become either overindulgent or too strict, often confused about the limits and rules they set. Inconsistency often becomes the pattern. When this happens, children experience a sense of insecurity because they are being given confusing signals about how they should live. Whatever the boundaries are for us and our children, they must be clear to every member of the family.

Constructing the boundaries for our families is a lot like building a fence around a yard. Boundaries help us keep the things that nurture us *inside* the fence and keep the things that would harm us *outside* the fence. We must be sure to stake out the land and define the rules in a way that gives our family a healthy context of what is right and wrong while at the same time giving family members the freedom to develop self-discipline and healthy standards for living. Good boundaries actually make kids feel good because boundaries help them know what is expected of them. They know what "good" looks like and can consciously choose it.

In a sense, this business of boundaries is a spiritual discipline. It's a way of staying in tune with the God-given design for the universe. It is not an accident that when Jesus taught us to pray, he taught us to ask God to "forgive us our trespasses as we forgive those who trespass against us." Violating God's laws and sinning against our neighbor are issues of mistaken boundaries, confused property lines. Trespasses occur when we do not have a clear picture about the rules and order for living.

How Do We Discipline Our Children?
**Your parenting style always boils down to
how you use your authority over your children.**
KEVIN LEMAN

NEAR the end of our son Chris's senior year in high school, he went on an outing with the choir to participate in a music festival. One night some of the students somehow acquired some beer and planned a secret party on the beach. Chris knew that what was about to happen was a violation of the rules, and he also knew that the chances of getting caught were great.

He tried to warn his friends not to go ahead with this party. Chris attended the party, but to his credit, he did not drink. Instead, he tried to encourage his friends not to participate. He was not entirely successful, especially with the girl whom he had planned to take to the high school prom the next week. Sure enough, the choir director discovered the beer party. The students were brought home before the festival was finished. Some of the kids who participated were suspended from school. When I heard the news, I was both proud and upset. The choir director told me that Chris had been an influence in trying to help stop the party and had convinced some of the kids not to drink. I was proud that Chris had stood up for the right thing, but I was upset that the girl he was planning to take to the prom had been involved in drinking. In my haste and without thinking through my rationale, I told Chris that he should not go to the prom with this girl. Since it was too late for him to get another date and since he didn't want to hurt this girl by going with someone else, he (and she) missed the prom.

Inadvertently I had punished Chris for doing the right thing. Later I realized that I should have let Chris make his own decision about the prom. It hurt Chris. While he did not say anything at the time, he felt that my decision was wrong. It robbed him of his high school prom, an event that happens only once in a kid's life. Later when Chris was a freshman in college, I wrote him a letter to apologize.

How to administer the boundaries is *the* hot button with most parents. What parameters should we set? How do we do the rule-discipline thing successfully? How do we apply it fairly? How do we temper and change it as our children grow? What is acceptable behavior, and what is not? As a parent, how do I keep my sanity, channel my frustration, harness my anger, enforce the rules, and act lovingly all at the same time? It is not an easy proposition. It is a difficult calling, one filled with a great deal of anxiety and self-doubt, even for the best of parents.

It takes some careful thought to consider what our boundaries should be: What is the structure we need in order to develop whole children? Are our boundaries flexible enough to let growth happen? Are we applying them fairly? This becomes more difficult when we consider that each person in the home is in the process of living, discovering, learning, and growing—including us, the parents.

Discipline is one area in which *all* parents feel frustration about how to do it right. We wonder how to make our children obey, how to get them to clean their rooms, how to teach them values without sounding like a broken record, how to get them to do their homework without turning into a monster. Even more, we wonder how to get them to begin to demonstrate self-discipline, love, and service.

We face lots of questions: How fast should we bolt from a deep sleep to tend to the screaming baby in the crib? Do we permit our son to wage food war from his high chair? Is the two-year-old allowed to slap Mommy when he's mad? Does our toddler have a right to make our shopping trip into a horror show? Should two brothers, eight and ten, be allowed to "duke it out" to solve a dispute? Should a fifth grader be forced to do homework? Should a fourteen-year-old be allowed to go on a date? All of us face these questions if we have kids. It is normal to feel some anxiety about how to handle these and a thousand other situations like them.

Discipline literally means training that is expected to produce a specific character or pattern of behavior. Discipline is not just punishment, and it is not just a method of bringing the parent peace of mind. Good discipline shapes and molds children for good. It helped me to view discipline as setting limits and enforcing some form of consequence for breaking those limits.

Most homes have two kinds of rules: spoken rules and unspoken rules. Unspoken rules are unfair rules because they are not clearly laid out to children. Living with unspoken rules is like having land mines in the home. Children never know when they will step on one of these land mines with the resulting parental explosion. When the rules are fair and clearly laid out, including the consequences for breaking them, then boundaries become a source of order, security, and unity. They promote harmony because everyone knows what is expected.

When my children were young, I thought that children responded better to loud verbal threats of physical punishment than to any other form of discipline. "If you don't [name the desired activity], then I'm going to spank you!" The more intense I became in my threats, the better results I thought I was getting. The trouble was that without realizing it, I kept adding a decibel or two to my tone of voice and one more warning before I took action. This resulted in my becoming a screamer and my children ignoring me until I reached a certain level of frenzy, which signaled it was time act. To put it plainly, this created a negative disciplinary environment. The focus became my behavior rather than a set of clear rules for living. The rule became "Do whatever Dad wants when he reaches the frenzy point."

If you are like me, you will at some point during your parenting experience feel some frustration, confusion, and conflict, if not an outright I'm-at-my-wits'-end emotion about the relationship between you and your children. Consider several basic boundaries:

First, our children deserve the right to know what the

rules are. No rule should be an unspoken rule, and no child should be disciplined for breaking rules that are not clearly defined. Boundaries and the resulting consequences of violating them should be clear and overt.

Second, five or six major rules are enough. I should not set down so many rules that my children have trouble remembering what they are. Too many rules are like government regulations—thousands of pages only lawyers read.

Third, rules should include not only "don'ts" but also "do's." Our "do's" might include chores and homework rules; our "don'ts" might include unacceptable behaviors such as lying or using verbal put-downs.

Fourth, rules and their enforcement should be applied consistently and fairly to everyone in the house. Never play favorites! And if we parents break a rule, we should have the courage to confess and take the consequences. Remember that we are not always right just because we are the parents.

Fifth, be flexible. When the rules are not working smoothly, make some adjustments. Boundaries need to be flexible enough to change as our children mature. Flexibility also means that rules are tempered with grace and applied with love. Experience taught me that rules and discipline without love are empty, hollow, and menacing.

Catherine the Great, empress of Russia, said, "I praise loudly, I blame softly." That's good advice. It helped me when I became aware of the intensity of my criticism. No matter how important the point I was making, I discovered that if I chastised my children in anger, they remembered the emotion more than the message. For many children, the strong and compelling urge to live intimately and securely with their parents is frustrated and even blocked by attitudes of anger and control. We need to ask ourselves: Are we parents who are in control, or are we controlling parents?

Parents who are in control set good boundaries and limits, negotiate when necessary, hold the line when necessary, remain flexible enough to change the boundaries when it is appropriate, listen often, try not to lower themselves to bouts of anger, and do not resort to violence. They know how to draw the line in the sand and how to administer consequences without becoming angry or abusive.

Remember that good discipline is applied as an external boundary. The goal is to keep external boundaries in place until children develop their own boundaries. Boundaries are like the stake that supports the young willow tree. The stake is there for a specific purpose: to help the sapling grow straight. But once the tree has grown to be thick and straight, it no longer needs the boundaries of the support stake.

Controlling parents, on the other hand, don't know when to relax boundaries. They feel they must dominate and intimidate in order to control. They often operate from feelings of fear or anger. Often these come from deep wounds from their own childhood. Controlling parents are interfering parents. They overparent and overdiscipline. Their number one priority is respect—not earned by love, but demanded by threats. This is immature parenting.[5]

What type of discipline is right when it comes to consequences for violating the rules? I cannot answer that for you. So much depends on you, the temperament of your children, the severity of the violation, and similar factors. Eventually I added a variety of methods to my arsenal of disciplinary tools, including times for quietness, discussion, and restitution. I learned to withhold privileges, reward for positive responses, restrict my children's time with friends. At times I even spanked them.

Christian parents differ in their views of spanking as an appropriate disciplinary tool. Some parents have strong aversions to spanking children at any time. Others use it as the only form of discipline. I'm concerned when I hear that some Christian teachers advocate spanking children for almost any infraction. I find that scary.

When my children were younger, I spanked them a lot. But I have since come to believe that my method was not healthy. While I am not totally against spanking, I have come to believe I used spanking far more than it was necessary, especially with our first two children. If you have decided that spanking is an acceptable form of discipline, be sure to follow some basic rules. Experience has led me to adopt the following personal guidelines:

First, spanking should be used as a last resort, not a first resort. By that I mean it should not be the common way you discipline for every situation. If you use it frequently for small misbehaviors, it will lose its significance. Try other things before resorting to spanking, and use it for the big and obviously defiant violations, not the petty stuff.

Second, before you spank, give yourself time to think. Put some space between the violation and the discipline. Cool down if you are angry. It is important *never* to spank children when you are angry. Physical abuse can result when you are angry. Plus, like my children, yours might concentrate on your anger instead of the behavior that needs correction.

When you put some time into thinking about your decision, it puts things in perspective, and you are better able to decide if the severity of the punishment is appropriate.

Third, talk to your children calmly before the spanking. Make sure your children understand the reason for the spanking. Make certain they understand the rule they broke and why the consequence is spanking. Children should not be spanked for breaking unspoken rules. Never use spanking as a way to *teach* a rule. If spanking is used, it should always be for a defiant or willful violation of a major rule that children already clearly understand.

Fourth, it doesn't take several swats to make your point. The goal of discipline is to apply light, not heat. Apply spanking only to the degree necessary to make the consequential point. And remember that children differ. Some children never need to be spanked. If the parents are in control and the boundaries are clear, even the most strong-willed children will need less spanking. Never hit or punch your children with your hands or slap them on the head or in the face. Physical discipline should be administered only to the soft fleshy part of the buttocks.

Fifth, hug your children when you are finished. Let them know you love them. Affirm their good qualities and encourage their desire to do what's right. Pray with your children. I have learned to be careful not to force my kids to "promise never to do that again." That is an unrealistic promise, and children feel shame when the promise is broken. They might also think that promises are not significant commitments. I simply asked them to do their best in trying not to repeat the wrong behavior.

Remember to align your passions and pick your battles carefully. All parents should have some areas in which they lay down the rules and stand firm: These are *nonnegotiables*. But be careful that not everything is non-negotiable. Anchor your nonnegotiables in virtues and values. As I have gotten older, I have found fewer and fewer things in my nonnegotiables basket. Some things I used to think were nonnegotiable have gone into the let's-discuss-it-and-come-to-a-mutual-understanding basket. And with the things left in the nonnegotiables basket, I have learned to say no with a compassionate smile rather than a stern look of anger.

Some parents wage war with their children over such things as eating vegetables, brushing their teeth, keeping their rooms neat, and a thousand other distractions. It's good to ask yourself, "What issues are life-forming and therefore consequential for my children's future? What issues are not essential?" The issues you are willing to go to the mat for may not necessarily be keeping clean bedrooms, eating broccoli, and being in bed by nine o'clock. I decided to pick my battles and show my resolve on those issues that count for character development and spiritual growth. Otherwise, I tended to use up my emotional bank on things that didn't really count.[6]

As writer and mother Valerie Bell says in her book *Getting Out of Your Kids' Faces & into Their Hearts,* "There is room for passion in family life, but it must be passion for people. If we care deeply about anything, it must be for the ones in our care. We must guard against anything that would threaten healthy family relationships."[7]

✎ Allowing Children to Suffer Consequences
The surest way to make it hard for your children is to make it soft for them.
WESLEYAN METHODIST MAGAZINE

MAYBE you've heard the story about the boy who was watching a moth struggle to release itself from a cocoon. The boy couldn't bear to see the moth struggle, so he got some scissors and clipped the edges of the cocoon to make it easier for the moth to be released. However, rather than having helped the moth, the boy's actions damaged the moth. When it came out of the cocoon, it could not fly because its wings would not extend properly. The boy later discovered that moths need to struggle in the cocoon because the movement pumps into the wings the fluid necessary for them to fly. By robbing the moth of the struggle, the boy unknowingly caused the moth's death.

I know a mother who could not stand to see her son struggle to make his own way on the basketball team. The fact that he was not a starter was, in her mind, a result of the coach's lack of good judgment and prejudice against her son. She would not consider that perhaps her son was not as skilled a player as the boys who played first string. So the mother created a confrontation about it with the coach and with other parents.

She moved her son to three different schools while he was growing up because she blamed his teachers and the administration for his lack of progress. When her son was a teenager, she sued a Boy Scout group because her son broke his leg on a snow outing. It was not an accident in her mind; it was the fault of inadequate supervision of the group.

During most of this young man's life, he was smothered

by his mother's "protective" care. Now, in his twenties, he lives alone and rarely calls his mother. In fact, he avoids her incessant attempts to contact him and be with him. In a recent counseling session the mother tearfully said, "All I ever wanted to do was see that my children had a fair chance in life, and now they hate me for it."

We all know the urge we feel when our children are in trouble. It's instinctive to want to rescue them from adversity. Whether we are tempted to do tasks that they should do for themselves or to defend them against others or to bail them out of a crisis, we want to make life easier for them.

Trying to eliminate consequence is not the way to see that our children have a fair chance in life. As pastor Earl Palmer said, "We must prepare the child for the road, not the road for the child."[8] To criticize a schoolteacher for the way he or she dishes out homework assignments or handles a disciplinary situation or ignores your children's lack of effort is an attempt to rescue your children from having to face consequences. When we do this, we teach our children that somebody else is to blame for their failure.[9]

Someone tells the story of meeting a farmer after a dry spring and commenting about how hard the weather must be on the crops. The farmer replied, "Actually, the dry weather has been good for the plants in some ways. If they have too much rain, their roots may stay only on the surface. But the dryness causes the roots to go down deep to find moisture. In the end, the plants that have not had it so easy in the beginning fare better because their deep root system allows them to withstand storms later on."

When children have everything done for them and everything given to them, they do not develop deep roots of character. In this environment, they cannot learn from failure, appreciate the reward of personal achievement, learn self-discipline, and learn to fend for themselves. They will end up being far more unhappy than they would be if allowed to suffer some pain and adversity. They will blame their parents for their inability to mature as adults.

My dad used to say, "Adversity introduces a man to himself." Naturally we want to protect our children and to provide for them. But we need to resist the temptation to do too much, thereby robbing our children of important opportunities for growth.

The big buzzword today in raising children is *self-esteem*. The idea, promoted by child-rearing experts since the seventies, is that making children feel good about themselves is the most important quality we can give them. As a result, parents feel that one of their major responsibilities is to heap praise and attention on their children. But some experts say we have gone overboard in this approach. Family counselor John Rosemond says, "Assisting children toward the discovery of true self-esteem requires that parents create family environments that communicate the Three R's of respect, responsibility, and resourcefulness. In the family, parents, not children, should command center stage."[10] As one teacher put it, "Today's child is self-absorbed, often does no more than it takes to just get by, and gives up almost immediately if a problem even looks hard."[11] Real self-esteem develops when children find out that in spite of adversity, pain, fear, or even failure, they are capable of finding solutions and making their own way to success. Parents should see themselves as cheerleaders, facilitators, and supporters—not as rescuers. Parents cannot and should not do for children what they need to do for themselves.[12]

Sometimes we get confused about the value of consequences. Some parents think of negative consequences only in the context of punishment. While negative consequences may be the *result* of wrong behavior, their value is in their ability to teach us how to live and alter our future behavior. Negative consequences are not always bad. If they teach us what we need to learn and we improve from them, they are good even though they may be painful.

Sometimes bad things just happen. Floods and automobile accidents are not necessarily the result of wrong behavior, even though our human nature wants to assign some kind of blame on the negative events of life. These kinds of consequences are part of life, and our kids should see them as part of the life-isn't-always-fair category.

When consequences are viewed as results that can teach us how to live and apply life's lessons so we can become better people, they become a positive experience in our lives. But when they are used as threats or viewed as punishment, the natural instinct is to want to avoid them. When this happens, we tend to fear trying new things. Our goal then becomes to avoid pain rather than to seek truth and opportunity.[13]

When we teach our children the principle of consequences, we are also teaching them to have the courage to own up to their behavior and mistakes and to draw commonsense conclusions about which behaviors are wrong. Courage means we do the right thing even when it carries a personal price tag, a personal consequence we may not enjoy.

✒ Letting Go

**Hold everything in your hands lightly—
otherwise it hurts when God pries your fingers open.**

CORRIE TEN BOOM

THE GOOD ground of the healthy home also prepares children—and their parents—to move beyond the boundaries of childhood. The day Jon, our oldest son, left home for college is vividly embedded in my mind. I had been preparing myself for this day for a long time, knowing that it was coming, that it should come. I tried to see it as a passage that brought a sense of pride and accomplishment in a son who had already demonstrated strong characteristics of self-preservation and leadership.

Jon was going off to a college in California. He had been a good student, a varsity basketball player, a good Christian witness, a student-body leader, and a loving son. He had goals, optimism, character, and ambition. What more could a father ask? And I *was* proud. I had purposed in my heart that this warm August morning of departure would be one of celebration. But it didn't happen quite that way.

Inside of me that morning was a sense of loss I could not escape. Something told me that a part of our life together was over forever and that I would never again have with Jon what I had now. I tried to console my grieving with thoughts of a new relationship between us—one that would be less father-to-son and more friend-to-friend. But my heart refused to cooperate with my rationale. My heart kept up its emotional hemorrhaging, and all of the mental arguments just didn't quash the anguish deep within.

The final moment had come. There was Jonathan, in his

little Dodge Colt packed to the roof with his belongings. He rolled down his window for one last good-bye. Nancie did the usual mother things, like asking, "Do you have any Kleenex? Did you get the lunch I packed? Do you have your gas money handy?" Both of us reminded him to drive carefully. We just hung around outside his window, awkwardly trying to prolong these final awful moments.

What else could I say, looking at this flesh of my flesh and bone of my bone, our first offspring, revving his engine, glowing with excitement and optimism, eager to birth himself on the road of his future, while I, like a wounded soldier knowing he must amputate his leg in order to survive, tried to cut the last tiny strings of adolescent attachment from my bleeding heart?

I reached through the window one more time to hug his neck. "I love you, Son, and I am very proud to be your dad," I said in a halting voice. His mother, now weeping openly, kissed his neck one more time.

"I've gotta get going now," he said, as if knowing that if he did not take the initiative to leave, his two grieving parents would stand there forever repeating what had already been said a hundred times.

Jon reached into his duffel bag on the floor of his car and handed each of us a letter he had written. "I love you, Mom and Dad. I'll call you when I get to Redding, okay?" We waved, unable to speak as his car eased out of the driveway and down the street on a trip that would take him six hundred miles away—and even further into our new relationship, one that none of us had ever experienced before. Nancie and I stood there together and wept until our heads ached as we

read the sweet letters of love and thanks he had so thought-
fully crafted for each of us the night before.

Letting go is one of the hardest things I have faced as a
parent. Nancie and I have had to do it several times now, and it
has never gotten any easier.

As Nancie wrote in her journal after one of our kids'
departure, "How does a parent mark the loss of childhood?
There are no Hallmark cards for such occasions. You sort the
pictures and memories into scrapbooks. You love them, and
you smile into the future as you let them go."

But letting go is an important part of the transition from
parent-imposed boundaries to self-imposed boundaries.
Every fence must have a gate. As children grow, we remove
our boundaries piece by piece. In healthy homes, children
make the successful transition from the playpen to the backyard to the neighborhood to the world. Letting go means that
as we parents stop imposing and enforcing the rules, our children impose and enforce their own rules and boundaries.

Letting go means that from then on, the role of parent
undergoes a dramatic change. At the point we launch our
children into adult life—be it college, marriage, or any other
form of leaving the nest—we can only watch, pray, applaud,
advise when asked, and cultivate their friendship. And it happens by degrees over time. Jon's car exiting our driveway
that morning was the end of a rather lengthy process of letting him go.

The letting-go process is hard on children too. Their move
to independence, both physical and emotional, is often awk-
ward and disruptive. For them, leaving means becoming their
own persons. It takes some time. Getting used to the idea is

stressful for both parent and children. It is not as if children are dependent one day and independent the next.

Before Nancie's and my children actually took full flight, there was a lot of wing flapping going on in our nest. Some of it is still going on. It's messy business. Feathers fly everywhere. Feathers get ruffled. Everyone associated with the nest at these times feels some of the discomfort.

Part of the wing-flapping process makes our children look as if they are floundering. They flip-flop about their plans for the future. They express what seem to be foreign values. They will test the waters of ideas, really not having any clue about where they are supposed to end up. During this time, they will make some poor choices.

My temptation was to point out my children's flaws, telling them that they shouldn't waste their money on a new stereo or that they should work more and play less or that they sleep in too much or that they should pick their friends and their clothes more in keeping with my tastes. And to the boy-man or girl-woman seeking independence, this kind of advice always feels restrictive and stifling. It often requires them to challenge the values of their parents and try on new things before they fully know who they are.

They will act cranky and rebellious, mainly because they don't have any idea about what they really want or what they should be and they are tired of answering the incessant questions about their future. They know only that they must leave the nest and fly somewhere, somehow. And if we as parents clutch, cling, demand, or probe too much during these times, we can damage the long-term relationship and cripple our children.

Mother and writer Polly Berrien Berends says in her book *Gently Lead,* "A child needs both to be hugged and unhugged. The hug lets her know she is valuable. The unhug lets her know that she is viable. If you're always shoving your children away, they will cling to you for love. If you're always holding them close, they will cling to you for fear."[14]

Most parents begin to feel the pain of letting go during the teen or preteen years, when the boundaries we have set up feel restrictive and stifling to our children and we are in a state of confusion and grief about how to let them go. Before our children become adolescents, they protest, but we parents clearly have the upper hand. But when our children hit adolescence, something inside of them shouts, "Enough!" Our children's developmental clock is going off on schedule, and they are needing some freedom. If we are wise parents, we will recognize this as a natural process rather than the signs of rebellion. We should then begin to provide outlets for their need for freedom and independence. We do this by changing the boundaries, even removing many of them. A fenced-in backyard is no longer big enough. The letting-go process is much easier for everyone if its natural stages are honored.

Of course, parents must decide which freedoms are reasonable and which are not. Children will always push for more. We must decide which rules and boundaries need alteration and which must remain steadfast. But we must do this not out of our own insecure clinging but out of a mature understanding of the process of growing up.

When our anxieties and clinging are in overdrive, we lose our ability to discern between which boundaries and freedoms are reasonable and which are unreasonable. We then become controlling parents.

If we do not give our children the chance to grow up, if we are unwilling to take the necessary risks, we start smothering our children. Anyone who feels smothered will fight to be released enough to breathe again. As someone has so aptly said, "Parents need to know the difference between holding a hand and chaining a soul."[15]

For many parents, their children define their lives and give meaning to their existence. They feel the satisfaction of knowing that their children depend on them. But that often means that when their children grow up, parents feel they lose personal meaning.[16] That's what is meant by the "empty-nest syndrome."

In a sense, overparenting is a form of addiction. Like the alcoholic or workaholic, we cannot stop being too much the parent. Addicted parents seem to have no identity outside of their children. These parents are either unwilling or unable to let go. The irony is that by refusing to let go as natural human development demands, we tend to destroy the very relationship and love we so desperately want to preserve.

One of the reasons some parents may not be able to let go is that they have not yet dealt with their own mortality. We do not see ourselves as passing from the scene, and, therefore, we do not see our children as the ones to whom we are passing the torch. Once we see our own fragile mortality, the fierce love we feel for our children will drive us toward making them able to stand on their own.

I wish I could offer some easy steps for letting go of your

children. I am still in the process, and I find the going a challenge. In a way, we parents must view ourselves as the ground crew with some previous flight experience of our own. We are the ones fueling the craft, helping to map the flight, checking the wings, and clearing the runway. But we are not the ones taking flight. We are the ones watching our children soar into the sky. Philosopher Kahlil Gibran once said, "You are the bows from which your children as living arrows are sent forth. The Archer sees the mark upon the path of the infinite, and He bends you with His might that His arrows might go swift and far. Let your bending in the Archer's hand be for gladness; for even as He loves the arrow that flies, so He loves also the bow that is stable."[17]

We will feel the letting-go emotions often—when our children take their first steps; when they go to kindergarten for the first time; when they begin to drive the car; at milestone birthdays, graduations, and weddings. It will always be a bittersweet experience to feel the ongoing separation.

BOUNDARIES, like fences, give our ground a definition. When we have good boundaries, we know where we are. They are reference points, landmarks for living. When we have clear boundaries, we help our children stay planted in the good ground we've provided. These boundaries will help our children grow physically, emotionally, morally, spiritually, ethically, and relationally. Remember that discipline is the way to teach and enforce the boundaries when our children are young. But the larger goal is to help our children set good boundaries for themselves and for their own offspring.

TILLING THE GROUND
Questions for Thought and Reflection

As you think about how you can practice the habit of making your home a place of boundaries, record your thoughts in a journal or notebook. Then share your reflections with your spouse or a close friend, asking them to pray for you and help you to put into practice some of the things about which you have been convicted.

1. What are the written and unwritten rules in your house? Do you have more than five or six major rules?

2. Does each person in your household know clearly what these rules are? Are the rules fair and consistently applied to everyone?

3. In what ways have the boundaries changed as your children have matured?

4. Do you consider yourself an effective disciplinarian? If yes, what makes you good at it, and if no, what are your weaknesses? How can you and your spouse improve your disciplinary practices? Have you ever disciplined in anger?

5. How do you and your spouse handle spanking? Do you agree or disagree with the spanking guidelines outlined in this chapter?

6. Recall a time when "suffering the consequences" ended up being a positive experience that taught you valuable lessons for living. How can living with the consequences help your children grow? What prevents you from allowing your children to suffer consequences? How can you keep from rescuing them?

7. When you were growing up, did you consider your parents too strict or too liberal? How did that affect you?

8. How has your experience as a child shaped your own parenting style? Have you set appropriate boundaries for your children?

9. What are your personal boundaries? Are you good at saying no and sticking to it?

10. What boundaries does God expect you to keep?

CHAPTER 5

Celebration
Is Life Good?

I want to be remembered as someone
who was fun to live with.

BILLY GRAHAM

🌿 Celebrating Life

**You are not only making memories—
you *are* the memories.**

VALERIE BELL

IF LIFE is to be joyful, we must be people who know how to celebrate. Celebration is a habit that will teach your children that life is essentially good. Home is the place of living and laughing. It should be the place we learn to play, to have fun, to relax.

Make sure that the good ground of your home includes an abundance of laughter, parties, celebrations, presents, candles, Christmas trees, gifts, surprises, rocky road ice cream, jokes, backyard picnics, vacations, mountain hikes, bike rides, swimming, fishing, and games. At the various houses in which our family has lived, we have had things like a swing set, a tree house, a tent, sleeping bags, a basketball hoop, baseballs, gloves, and bats.

As writer and pastor Peter Marshall once said, "God is a God of laughter, as well as of prayer . . . a God of singing, as well as of tears. God is at home in the play of His children. He loves to hear us laugh."[1] Celebration nourishes us. It is essential to our human experience, and we go out of our way to make it happen.

Celebration is a spiritual thing. The angel announced the coming of Jesus with jubilant words. "Don't be afraid!" he said. "I bring you good news of great joy for everyone!"[2] Jesus told his followers before he left them, "I have told you this so that you will be filled with my joy. Yes, your joy will overflow!"[3]

All of the important dates on the Jewish calendar are punctuated with feasts. Jesus began his public ministry at a wedding reception at which he saved the host, who had run out of wine, from embarrassment by turning water into the finest wine at the gathering. As writer and theologian Richard Foster puts it, "Celebration is central to all the Spiritual Disciplines. Without a joyful spirit of festivity the Disciplines become dull, death-breathing tools in the hands of modern Pharisees."[4] In her book *Jesus, CEO,* Laurie Beth Jones tells this story: "A ten-year-old once asked me if I knew what Jesus' first words were after he came out of the tomb. 'No,' I replied. 'What were they?' He spread his arms, jumped forward with a grin, and said, 'Ta-dah!'" Jesus was into celebration.[5]

Celebrations and traditions remind us that life is worth living. A celebration can curse despair by reminding us that there is joy in the world. Celebrations mark our growth and achievements, commitments and milestones. Our rites of passage are validated and honored in celebration.

For our family, celebration is something as simple as eating cold watermelon together on a hot day in our backyard and building a snowman six months later in the same backyard. We don't celebrate just holidays and events. We tend to celebrate whenever people come together. To have a birthday party without people around feels empty and cold. Where would national holidays be if it were not for the people who celebrate them? Where would the Super Bowl be if it were not for the crowds, the game, the winners, the hoopla, the tailgate parties, and the countless festivities? Would Christmas be the same without the wonder and twinkle of children around the tree? These events and holidays serve as reasons to gather us together in a joyous expression of community, tradition, and togetherness.

Celebration breaks the routine, relieves the stress, and provides a needed relief to life's pressures. When we celebrate, the daily song changes from a predictable humdrum to a vibrant rhapsody. The tempo picks up, and new singers join in the chorus. Celebration helps us reflect on what is essential, what is important. Celebration prevents us from taking life too seriously and helps us see our lives and those we live with in fresh ways.

Celebrating the Child

Children need more than food, shelter, and clothing.
The bottom line is: Every child needs at least one person who's crazy about him.
FRAN STOTT

MY GRANDMOTHER was my biggest cheerleader. Whenever she saw me coming, she lit up as if my presence was the best thing that happened in her day. When she looked at me, it always seemed to be a look of adoration and delight. She often told me that I was a special child and that God had special things for me to do. I loved being near her because whenever I was, I felt that I was the occasion for her celebration.

She loved to hear me sing. My parents tell me that from the time I was in a crib, I sang. When I was a little boy, I would sit in the front row of our little church and sing my lungs out. Once the song leader stepped down and quietly asked me if I would please sing a bit softer so others could be heard. But Grandma later told him that others should sing louder—not that I should sing softer—that when people worship God, they ought to do it with all the fervor they can muster. It gave me great confidence. I would turn around to look at her a few pews back. She would give me a wink of approval, and I sang more loudly than ever.

After that, I started singing some solos in church. When I sang, she would close her eyes and have a wide smile on her face. She was enthralled. Her favorites were "The Love of God" and "The Last Mile of the Way." I sang those songs until I knew them by heart.

I continued to sing through high school. Later, I won a college scholarship in voice, partly because of my grandmother's encouragement. She died when I was a freshman in college. Before she died, she asked my father to have me sing at her funeral. I came home and sang my grandma into her grave with both of her favorite songs. It was our last celebration together, and this time I celebrated her as she had celebrated me.

To celebrate our children means to delight in them. Just as plants need warm sunlight to grow, children thrive when they are watched and adored. "Look, Mommy!" is a plea for Mommy to celebrate the child's activity.

I sometimes notice subtle disappointments from parents. Children notice too. Some parents never carry their children's pictures with them. They do not speak in excited tones about their children. Their voices trail off as they describe a litany of problems like grades, attitudes, and physical abilities. I grieve when I hear this because I know that the children of these parents are not feeling celebrated. In her article "Hopes and Prayers," Joyce Maynard describes what happens to many of us. "We're so consumed with the feeding, the dressing, the buckling into car seats, the finding of bathrooms, and the counting of heads," she says, "that we sometimes forget that there is any greater mission to raising children than making sure the crusts are cut off the sandwiches and that everybody gets a balloon."[6]

After I finished my graduate degree, I took a job as a teacher of mentally retarded and multihandicapped children. Most of my work was with children labeled EMR (educable mentally retarded). Timmy, one of my students, was one of the best teachers I ever had. Timmy was a bundle of optimistic joy every day. Many of the other children would sit with their heads bowed, not wanting to attempt anything new. It was as if something had died inside of them long ago. They knew they were "dumb." Somewhere, significant people in their lives had drilled their disappointment into them.

But not Timmy. He knew he was special. He was a child eager to try anything new. *Failure* was not in his vocabulary. When he made a mistake, he would grin and try again. He was animated and curious. Everything, from a story to a field trip, was a grand occasion. He made the entire classroom a fun place to be. He was an encourager. Many of the students began to try when Timmy loved them and encouraged them. The progress my students made was more the result of who Timmy was than what I did.

When I met his mother, I understood why. She came to school on Timmy's birthday to throw a surprise party for him. Dressed in a clown suit, she showed up with a huge cake, balloons, horns, hats, and small presents for every kid. Everything about her was gladness. Living with a retarded child had not broken her spirit. It was evident that Timmy was her great joy. She saw past his problems. She adored him for who he was. He was perfect just because he was Timmy.

I met the other parents too. Some of them could never imagine celebrating their children. These parents spoke in hushed, mournful tones. Their eyes did not light up. They allowed their overwhelming grief and disappointment to crush any good feelings they may have had for their child. Parents send messages to their children in many ways. When children sense our disappointment in them or our lack of joy about having them, they will internalize these signals, even when the signals are subtle.

Regardless of their abilities, children are miracles in the making. They are unique among us because they are works of God. The stages they go through will come only once during their rapid growth. Television host Art Linkletter made a small fortune interviewing little children because we adults delight in their expressions. We all love the annual school or Christmas program for kindergartners because we love their innocent antics. At times like these, most of us think children are simply adorable.

Special occasions are a form of celebrating children, but some celebratory adoration should be demonstrated every day. It is easy to get caught up in our children's development skills like reading and math. We have become so focused on achievement that we push our children to develop quickly. We want them to be the first and the best at mental and physical skills. But when we push our children to excel in ways that rush their childhood, we rob them and us of much of the celebration. Joy comes not only in the *doing* but also from *being.* *Doing* is usually related to performance, while *being* is related simply to who we are. As musician Pablo Casals once said, "Each second we live is a new and unique moment of the universe, a moment that will never be again. . . . And what do we teach our children? We teach them that two and two make four, and that Paris is the capital of France. When will we also teach them what they are? We should say to each of them: Do you know what you are? You are a marvel. You are unique. In all the years that have passed, there has never been another child like you."[7]

It is a wonderful thing to be excited about your children. When they say, "Look, Mommy!" don't say, "Shhhh, be quiet!" Instead, get excited with them. Enter their world of wonder, and let their enthusiasm and joy become yours as well. Running and laughing with your children will make your heart joyful, your mind pure. When you celebrate children, you are doing the work of God. It is a holy act. Jesus celebrated the children. He said, "Let the children come to me. Don't stop them! For the Kingdom of God belongs to such as these."[8]

Celebrating our children means we recognize that they are priceless. Their openness, their innocence, their simplicity, their lack of pretense, and their sense of faith and hope speak of the goodness we adults want to see manifested in us. Children remind us of God, and if for no other reason than this, we need to celebrate them.

🌿 Celebrating with Imagination
The best way to capture a child's imagination is to set it free.
UNKNOWN

ANDY and I had just finished saying our nighttime
prayers together. The next morning would be Easter Sunday.
We have a special celebration on Easter Sunday morning at
our house. Not only do we place an Easter basket full of good-
ies at the bedsides of our children, we hide little gifts around
the house for them to find, things Nancie and I feel are significant, like Bible storybooks, posters with character messages
on them, and a few other fun things like kites or Nerf balls.
It's like a scavenger hunt. When the children find one item,
they also find a note giving them a clue about where to look to
find the next item.

Just as we hugged good night, Andy looked me in the eyes
and said, "Dad, is there really an Easter bunny?"

Here I was, the publisher of a parenting magazine, the
"advice man," sitting at the bedside of my six-year-old son, at
a loss for words. It caught me by surprise. We had never made
a big deal about these pretend characters at our house, but
Andy's face was serious.

My mind raced. Was this a moment of real truth? Was this
for my child a theological question? Santa Claus, the Easter
bunny, and the tooth fairy were all fun little fantasy guys to
add imagination to our celebrations, but did Andy really
know it's only make-believe?

If I destroyed the make-believe about the Easter bunny,
I knew Santa and the tooth fairy would go down with him. In
make-believe terms, it seemed a shame to take down Santa
and the tooth fairy just because some bunny wanted to con-

fess. I decided to tell the truth, not the make-believe truth, but the real truth.

"Andy, you know we do some things just as fun little traditions," I said.

"What's a tradition?" he interrupted.

"Well, it is something we pass on to our kids because we did it when we were kids. Easter bunnies kind of fall into that category." I eased into it. "There are make-believe stories that we all go along with just because they add fun to a holiday or special occasion. Are you sure you want to know everything about the Easter bunny?"

"Yes," he said without hesitation.

"There is no *real* Easter bunny," I starkly whispered. "He's like the cartoon characters on television, like Mickey Mouse and Donald Duck, just make-believe." Andy lay silent for a moment, staring at the ceiling. I could almost hear his little mind mulling over what I had just told him.

"So you and Mom are the ones who put the Easter baskets out at night and hide all the stuff around the house?" he asked.

"Yes," I answered. "Does that make it less special?"

"No, Dad." He grinned. "I could never figure out how one little bunny carried all those baskets into our house anyway. Bunnies don't have hands, you know."

Then Andy did a wonderful thing. Just when he could have sentenced all these little characters into exile, he said, "Let's keep pretending anyway, okay, Dad?" I assured him that we would as we hugged good night. The world of make-believe would survive another year.

As I left the room, I thought how grateful all these make-believe characters ought to be feeling about now.

Andy had given them a reprieve, a pardon for being fake. He had decided to continue to hold citizenship in the world of imagination. *Somewhere,* I mused, *is a bearded fat man, a big-eared rabbit, and an odd-looking little dude in leotards breathing a sigh of relief.* Imagination is a wonderful thing.

As novelist Madeleine L'Engle once said, "Jesus was not a theologian but a God who told stories."[9] Imagination helps us know God. When we use our imagination, we can picture him better, receive his grace and love, and view life the way he intended. As C. S. Lewis put it, imagination is "the organ of meaning."[10] In her book *Imagination,* Cheryl Forbes says, "All the information we receive about God, our responsibility as his stewards, our roles as husbands, wives, sons, daughters, siblings, employers, or employees are so much dust without imagination to help us act on the information. Imagination is, to borrow a phrase from the Book of Common Prayer, our means of grace and our hope of glory. It humanizes us in the truest meaning of that word—by making us more like Christ, the only completely imaginative person who ever lived."[11]

Imagination is an important part of celebration. Stories, traditions, and myths add a sense of delight to many of our celebrations. Use your imagination when you tell a story to your children, like adding interesting details to the story of Jesus' birth at Christmas. "Imagine what the shepherds must have felt when they saw the angels and heard the incredible announcement of Jesus' birth. Imagine the angels as they silently watched the King of kings being born in a manger. Imagine the celebration in heaven! I think the angels were

dancing and shouting for joy! All the little stars twinkled as if
they were laughing in a grand chorus of gladness."

Imagination adds flavor to our celebrations. Children's
imaginations are especially keen, and they love to be told
stories that use their imaginative powers. Using imagination
is a way to convey important truth.

✥ Celebrating with Laughter and Play
**If you're not allowed to laugh in Heaven,
I don't want to go there.**
MARTIN LUTHER

EVERY family should have its own private jokes and
funny stories. Private jokes are never as funny to others
as they are to you, but they represent a shared hilarious
moment. They remind family members of the idiosyncrasies
and quirks of what happened. Often it takes only a word or
phrase of the joke to conjure up a memory that produces
wild laughter among the family members who were there
when the joke first happened.

Family jokes and stories are personal, often private.
To others they may seem silly, even stupid. And that's what
makes them special. They become code words for belonging.
They are descriptions of people and events that only you who
are connected as family can really understand and appreciate.
Family jokes and funny stories let you in. You become an
insider with the group, the inner circle, part of something
personal and unique.

One family story that my children enjoy telling happened
at my oldest son's wedding. My niece attended and brought

her three-year-old son, Weston. Weston's father is in his thirties and very physically fit. He's the all-American type who works out and has body definition and tight abdominal muscles. He used to be one of those guys who went around busting concrete blocks with his hands and head.

I, on the other hand, am a fifty-three-year-old pudge, and that's a compliment. During the wedding reception, Weston was spending some time with me. He was leaning on me, and I was hugging him while we carried on a simple conversation. Two of my own children were sitting with us, enjoying the moment.

Weston began to poke at my stomach. He was fascinated by the soft rolls that were so elastic and resilient. He would push his fingers in further and further, each time seeing the soft tallow bounce back to its original position. He had never touched a stomach like this before. He was fascinated. My children were grinning as they watched him. Pretty soon Weston looked up at me, dead serious, and said, "What's this for?"

My children nearly passed out laughing. They were rolling on the floor! Since then, on many occasions, my children have come up to me, affectionately poked my stomach, and said, "What's this for?" It always brings a laugh. Sometimes in public, given the right circumstance, they will say, "What's this for?" And the family, the insiders, instantly know what they are thinking.

Insider stories are a part of the intimate celebration that family members share in unique and special ways. We know these people well, and we can laugh with each other and at ourselves because we know they love us in spite of our flaws.

Children also *need* parents to play with them. Play is a

powerful source of celebrative connection. "Will you play with me?" means much more than just "Let's do a game." Children asking this question are asking for connection. They want to know you, touch you, and feel love between you. Playing brings us together in a magic way. When a father lies down on the floor to giggle, growl, and wrestle—playing monster one minute and Prince Charming the next—he is giving a priceless gift to his children. Playing and laughing is a pure form of getting down on the level where your children live. Play is important because it is a major building block in shaping relationships and experiencing the joy of celebration.

✥ Celebrating with Song and Dance

**When it comes to parenting children—
it's always dancing season—
regardless of what else is happening . . .
even if we must occasionally dance with a limp.**
VALERIE BELL

PASTED on my memory forever is the scene of my eighty-three-year-old father at his grandson's wedding reception, doing a crazy dance with his granddaughter. It was like a wild abandon of joy, and we all remember this moment as a family treasure. My dad was raised in a conservative home, and none of us had ever seen him dance before. Then, at age eighty-three, he was jivin' to the music of "Y-M-C-A." Our mouths hung open in disbelief! Soon we were all dancing with him.

Have you ever noticed that children often dance when they celebrate? It is like rhythm in their bones. When the music plays, most children will try to keep the beat in dance almost as early as they can walk. At times we parents need to practice a sense of abandon, let down our guard, loosen our neckties, take off our shoes, roll up our pant legs, and get into the celebration.

Remember that your children are receiving emotional cues from you about life. If you teach them how to sing and dance, you will be teaching them that joy is there in spite of life's curveballs. As ethics professor Lewis Smedes wrote in *Shame and Grace,* "If all must be right with the world before I may have a fling with joy, I shall be somber forever."[12]

There is enough grief and sorrow to go around, and we never know when it will visit our doorstep. That's why it's good to seize the moments of joy and celebration when they present themselves. Moments of joy are like a mystery. We never know for sure when they will happen, but when they do, they often come in like little dancing feet, surprising and delighting us. Their frequency will increase if you make song and dance a part of your life and celebrations.

✒ Celebrating Contentment
Beware! Don't be greedy for what you don't have.
LUKE 12:15

IF WE want to have healthy homes that know how to celebrate, we will need to find contentment along the way. The press for more, the race for what's newer, larger, and better only stresses us and our children. If we live our lives for a future moment, if we wait to take a vacation for a time when we can "afford" it, if we put our time and energy into building

a future life rather than the one we have now, we will miss the
joy of living with our children while they are growing up.

When Nancie and I started our magazine-publishing company, we had to mortgage our house to have enough money to
begin the business. It was rough going the first few years, and
some weeks we were not sure we would even make payroll. I
used to pray, "God, if you will just give us enough money to
have a $1,000 cushion in the bank, I would be grateful."
When we did reach that goal, my prayer had changed. I was
asking God for a $10,000 cushion because by then our obli-
gations were much larger. When we reached that goal, my
prayer was for a $100,000 cushion. I never felt completely
contented, even though we always had enough money. We
paid our bills on time, and we never once missed payroll.

It is easy to miss life if we're always looking for another
one while trudging through the one we already have. This is
a real dilemma for many families. Our culture's obsession to
produce more leads to an obsession to acquire more. In the
process, it leaves many of us feeling discontented with who we
are and what we have. If we are stay-at-home parents, we feel
left out of life. If we have a 1989 automobile, we look toward
having a 1996 automobile. If we live in a two-bedroom house,
we cast our eye toward the three- or four-bedroom houses.
We fantasize about winning the ten-million-dollar sweep-
stakes. We want more, we want better, and we take pride in
the wanting. It is an affliction of our times.

Roger and Cindy, a couple in our church, are a good example of contentment. When they were married, they both held
full-time jobs outside the home. During that time they
planned for their family by putting away a small amount of

money while at the same time purchasing a small home. When Cindy was eight months pregnant with their first child, she quit her job to become a full-time mother.

That was eleven years ago, and she is still at home, giving most of her time to their three children. Roger has had a couple of promotions at his job, but a long time ago, he and Cindy got off the treadmill of striving for more. Roger had the opportunity to transfer to a larger city for a big promotion with the investment firm he works for as a broker, but it meant a long commute, much more travel, and time away from his family. He turned it down because he wants to be home more often while his kids are growing up.

Roger and Cindy live in a modest house and drive an older station wagon, but the attitude of contentment is evident with this family. They take inexpensive vacations by camping in the mountains, and they take day hikes. They attend all of their children's school activities, and they take an active role in church. In many ways, Roger and Cindy's celebration of contentment puts them way ahead of many other people who have put their family life on hold in order to be more financially successful.

Contentment is akin to simplicity. Contentment will bring gladness to our lives. The opposite of contentment is discontentment. Discontentment wakes us up with the nagging, gnawing sense of dissatisfaction. It makes us heavyhearted and envious. When we are not contented, we covet.

While achievement and excellence are noble pursuits, we can miss living a measured and contented life if we are always striving for something else. This is especially true while our children are growing up. Fathers often miss their children's vital years because they are busy building a career. In our pursuit of excellence, we must not forget to celebrate the joy of being a family, of parenting our children, and of being satisfied. Contentment brings a joy that nothing else can bring, but it is a joy that is hard to find unless we pay the price of giving up some of our striving.

Much of this kind of contentment comes from concentrating on simple, everyday blessings—laughing with our children, enjoying the sunshine, being truly thankful for food and shelter, appreciating a friend, expressing our love to those who need us, and spending time with God. It comes from taking one day at a time and appreciating that day as a gift. Someone has penned, "Yesterday is history. Tomorrow is mystery. Today is a gift. That's why we call it 'The Present.'"[13]

There is a real danger of missing life when we are always looking to the future for our contentment. Sometimes when our children are young, we dread the diaper routine and long for the day when our children will be potty trained. Then we look for the day they will start school. It is a vicious cycle: "First I was dying to finish high school and start college. And then I was dying to finish college and start working. And then I was dying to marry and have children. And then I was dying for my children to grow old enough for school so I could return to work. And then I was dying to retire. And now, I am dying . . . and suddenly I realize I forgot to live."[14] In healthy homes, parents and children celebrate The Present. They live in attitudes of contentment and simplicity, knowing that the time together as a family will be over sooner than they can imagine. Contentment may not come easily when you are down in the trenches parenting wiggly and noisy toddlers. But remember that parenting young children is a season of life, not a permanent state of life.

Many people miss life. It passes them by because they don't recognize it. Life is not a place, not a goal, not an event; it is a process. We sometimes view life as "getting there," and we think that once we get there, we will feel complete. The truth is that the process of getting there *is* life and that we will never "arrive" during this life. To view life as a process and to find joy in the journey is to celebrate contentment in our homes.

Having healthy homes with contentment is not an accident; it is an art. Contentment is a skill we practice, and we teach it to our children in the process. Contentment and gratitude are twin sisters. If you don't hone your skill at being grateful with what you have now, you will not be contented when you have more.

🌿 Celebrating with Traditions

Traditions identify us like a fingerprint. They anchor us.
If we did not have these particular traditions, we would have others.
That is because traditions insist upon themselves: Look around, and you will see them trying to exist everywhere, in everyone's life.
Clearly we need them.
ELIZABETH BERG

HERE'S the way it has to be done: The fresh-cooked clam chowder is made from scratch and is served with chilled prawns and Nancie's homemade rolls. That's the annual meal on Christmas Eve at our house. Before we eat, we listen to the Christmas story, each person reading a set of verses. Then we pray and thank God for the gift of his Son. After dinner, we open presents, one at a time, youngest to oldest, until all the presents are open. The next day, Christmas dinner is always prime rib. If that's not the way it's done, it ain't right! It's tradition!

Every family's traditions are different, but every family has them. Traditions have repetition to them. They have predictability. They are a stored treasure of memory. Like antiques, the older they get, the more priceless they seem. Traditions recall a part not only of our immediate past but also of everyone who is in our family tree. Keeping traditions keeps our memories alive.

There are levels of traditions. They range from broadly shared ones to highly intimate ones. National traditions and holidays are shared by millions. Religious and ethnic traditions are shared by those of similar faith or backgrounds. Family traditions are an even tighter circle and range from our extended family to our immediate family. Finally, there are personal and intimate traditions, sometimes shared with a spouse or even performed alone. In keeping our traditions, we pay homage to the rhythms of life.

Traditions are repeat performances that add joy from previous memories. Traditions carry deep significance, allowing us to be the conduit that builds on the past, linking it with the future. We are the *now* actors who play out the ritual we learned from our parents. We teach this in a way that connects our children to our family story. As one person described it, "To show a child what has once delighted you, to find the child's delight added to your own, so that there is now a double delight seen in the glow of trust and affection, this is happiness."[15]

Traditions are more than celebrating holidays like Thanksgiving and Christmas. Traditions can be built on simple acts and daily routines, like preparing a meal, eating together, saying grace together, doing chores together, and having family times together.[16] Daily things are the most constant traditions of our home. They are the things that give meaning and context to life. They help to define our present lives and become the signature of who we are. Traditions, like glue, bind and hold families together in unique and special ways. Children need these foundational rituals to reinforce the message that they belong, that their connection is deep and enduring.

It is easy in the routine of everyday life to ignore the significance of tradition. And yet it is these small daily things that tend to become some of the most powerful watermarks of our lives. Reading and telling stories at bedtime, back rubbing and cuddling, playing games and going on outings, taking pictures and keeping a scrapbook, praying together and attending church together are all ways we create tradition.

Because we live in times of rapid change, it is up to us parents to create the stability of tradition and ritual in our homes. We live in times of divorce and blended families. We live in times of job layoffs and frequent moves to new towns and states. We live in times when grandparents and other extended-family members may live thousands of miles away. It is vital that in the midst of this stress and chaos, we provide bedrock traditions to give an underpinning to our homes. We do this by making life—everyday life and special occasions—a celebration of traditions.

🌿 Celebrating with Ceremony

**What greater thing is there for human souls
than to feel that they are joined for life—
to be with each other in silent unspeakable memories.**

GEORGE ELIOT

ON AUGUST 20, 1966, in a little farming town in northern Montana, two wide-eyed young people did what countless others have done for centuries. Nancie and I recited age-old sacred vows "to love, honor, and cherish until death do us part." Mabel Bain, Nancie's childhood piano teacher, played the organ, and I sang a special song to my beautiful young bride. Uncle Kenny prayed a traditional prayer as both of our families and many of our friends looked on. Nancie and I both cried as we looked in each other's eyes and said, "I will."

Three years later in Santa Cruz, California, we stood before the man who had been my pastor when I was a child and handed him our firstborn infant son. Again we said "I will" to the challenge to raise our son to love the God we knew.

In the twenty-seven years since then, we have gone through four more child dedications, one ordination, five baptisms, four high school graduations, three college graduations, dozens of award ceremonies, two funerals, a twenty-fifth wedding anniversary, and one child's wedding. At times the going has not been easy, but we knew we meant what we said when we spoke our first ceremonial vows over thirty years ago.

Every so often, I take time to glance back at the ceremonies of my life. They rise up like landmarks to remind me of my commitments. When I line up these ceremonial landmarks, I always find them pointing me clearly in the direction I should head into the future. Ceremonies give witness to our promises and drive a stake into our commitments. They become stark reminders of what we claim is most important.

Your children are profoundly influenced by your ceremonies. Even before they are born, the vows you exchange will mean something to them in the future. When you give them back to God in infancy, you are making on their lives a divine claim that will have an influence on their future choices. As your children see you celebrate ceremonies and keep your commitments, they learn that celebration not only means joy but also has a context of deep significance. In the record of the Old Testament, God pronounced feasts to mark covenants with his people because he wanted them to remember his and their promises.

The promises we make in ceremony and our efforts to keep them become the essence of who we are. In the play *A Man for All Seasons,* Sir Thomas More is being tried for treason because he will not break his vow to the Church of England and compromise his principles to make it convenient for King Henry VIII to divorce and remarry. More's daughter, who knows that he will be convicted and sentenced to death, pleads with him to reconsider. Sir Thomas More says to her, "When a man makes a promise, Meg, he puts himself into his own hands, like water. And if he opens his fingers to let it out, he need not hope to find himself again." That is why we give our significant promises and take our oaths in ceremony. Ceremony solemnizes life's passages. Births, baptisms, graduations, weddings, and funerals are familiar ways we celebrate passages. Ceremony speaks of love and commitment, achievement and promise, life and death. Some ceremonies validate unspeakable joy; others validate unspeakable grief. All of them are very personal and deeply spiritual. They are at the core of our beliefs. Baptism is a ceremony celebrating our union with Christ. Weddings are witness to our vows and a celebration of union with our chosen beloved. Graduations are celebrations of achievement and the pursuit of our life's work and calling. Funerals celebrate a life completed.

Ceremonies help preserve our family foundations and give us milestones by which to measure our lives. Ceremonies help us pass on our values from generation to generation. They help us make the core elements of our homes stable and enduring. Our ceremonies become a drumbeat to which we walk the path of life. They are predictable passages into new lands.

It is as if we are cooperating with God in writing a novel, the novel of our life, and our ceremonies mark the chapters and keep track of the story line we are weaving into it. Ceremonies force us to pause and pay attention to where we are and the chapters we are writing now.

In the Old Testament book of Jeremiah, when Israel was going into exile, God encouraged his people to set up road signs pointing back to Israel. "Mark well the path by which you came," he said.[17] He knew that if they remembered where they had come from, they would find their way back. Allow your ceremonies and the ceremonies of your children to be the milestones and sacred moments that mark the path of life for you and your family.

LAUGH, cry, adore, and make a mountain of memories. Joy is like water when you're thirsty. You can drink and drink, but you'll always come back for more. Kick up your heels a bit, take time off, live your traditions, and keep your imagination alive. Give in to humor, but take your promises seriously. Celebrate every chance you get. This is your life, and now is the time to celebrate.

TILLING THE GROUND
Questions for Thought and Reflection

As you think about how you can practice the habit of making your home a place of celebration, record your thoughts in a journal or notebook. Then share your reflections with your spouse or a close friend, asking them to pray for you and help you to put into practice some of the things about which you have been convicted.

1. Do you feel that life for you has been essentially good? Why or why not?

2. Do you enjoy celebrating? How and when do you celebrate? What kinds of celebrations are your favorite and why? Who do you like being with when you celebrate? What people in your life have been good models of celebrating? What do they do to radiate joy to others?

3. What makes life special for your children?

4. How do you express joy *in* your children, *to* your children? Do your children feel special? What are some ways you could encourage your children more? How can you become your children's biggest "cheerleader"?

5. Do you push your children to achieve? If so, is it a healthy or unhealthy prodding? In other words, is it your dream you are pushing or is it their dream and giftedness you are helping them to realize? How is the prodding balanced with times of celebration?

6. Do you feel you are a contented person, a contented family? If yes, what makes you feel contented? If no, what is the source of your lack of contentment? In what ways do you balance your striving to reach goals with times of relaxation and celebration?

7. What could you do to help relieve stress in your family? in your children? Are you living life as if you enjoy the journey, or are you running to try to catch up to some other life you want to live?

8. What are your favorite traditions? Do you have daily and/or weekly traditions in addition to holiday traditions? What are they? What are some things you could do to strengthen your family's traditions?

9. What are the promises and commitments you are endeavoring to keep? How are you teaching your children the significance of keeping their promises?

10. What does God say about joy in his Word? In what ways does God want to bring joy to your life?

CHAPTER 6

Connection
Am I Loved?

The truth is that from the day we're born until the day we die,
we need to feel held and contained somewhere.
We can let go and become independent
only when we feel sufficiently connected to other people.

RON TAFFEL

🌿 Bonding with Our Children
To love and be loved is to feel the sun from both sides.
DAVID VISCOTT

THE NIGHT before our oldest son, Jonathan, was born, I took Nancie for a bumpy ride in the car to try to start her labor. She was tired of waiting. Her due date had come, and the doctor was ready to induce labor if it did not happen naturally. The bumpy car ride had no effect. It was as if our baby were stuck in the womb.

The next day we went to the hospital to have the labor induced. My parents and Nancie's parents joined me in the waiting room. I kissed Nancie as she was led into the delivery room. In those days, fathers were not permitted to be present at the birth.

I will never forget the swinging doors opening from the delivery room as the nurse brought a little blanket-wrapped bundle toward me and said, "Here is your new son." My huge grin turned to tears as I held Jonathan William, our first child. New grandmas were crying, and new grandpas were giggling. In a split second, my arms and heart held the object of my affection, and I knew that I would gladly die for him if need be.

This connecting miracle is a mystery to me. With our

other three sons, Eric, Chris, and Andy, that same connection began at the moment of birth.

I had some fear about whether it would happen the same with Amy, our adopted daughter. We were all standing in the SeaTac terminal when the Northwest Airlines 747 pulled up to the gate. We waited while the passengers, coming from Seoul, Korea, cleared customs. The boys were all excited to meet their newly adopted sister, and Nancie was ecstatic about having her first daughter.

I was anxious. I was worried that I would not be able to love this child in the way I loved our biological children.

A woman appeared, coming down the escalator and through the glass doors. Three-and-a-half-year-old Kim Yung Ja was handed to Nancie. The boys rushed to hug her. She was amused and confused. As I approached her, she screamed in terror, shrinking away. My worst fears were realized: This child was accepting Nancie and the boys, but she was rejecting me.

It turned out that she was raised by a *bomo,* or grandmother figure, and had had little contact with grown men. My rush toward her amid all the other excitement had frightened her. Our bonding would take some time. It was a mutual wariness.

The bonding began two nights later. Amy woke up in the night, grieving for her *bomo.* I heard her cry and picked her up. By then she would let me touch her, feeling I was safe after all. I sat in the rocking chair nearby and began to sing to her softly as I rocked her in my arms. As I sang, "Go tell Aunt Rhody her old gray goose is dead"—a crazy little song we sang to all of our children—she stopped crying and looked up into my eyes. I smiled at her. She reached up and touched my face and smiled back at me. In that moment, I felt what I had felt with each of my other children. That was twelve years ago, and my love for her has only continued to increase.

The other day Amy and I decided it was time for us to have a dad-daughter date. Actually it was her idea. I know that some fathers do this regularly, but while Amy and I do things together often, this was the first time we planned to have a date. "You can decide what we should do, Dad," she said. "I just want to be with you." Well, what father could resist an offer like that?

Amy loves to do "artsy" things. She loves drawing and painting and building paper mobiles and models. I noticed that the craft supply store was having a big sale, and I thought our date should include a trip there to pick out some paints or something that she would enjoy using creatively. After our dinner together, we headed for the store.

It was a big hit. In fact, we got so carried away with the 70-percent-off sale that we ended up with a whole new set of acrylic paints, an airbrush, and some how-to painting books.

Last night we finished our first project together. It was a cardboard model of Bachelor Butte, a local ski mountain, for Amy's science class. (We were both hoping to get an A since it really looks great!) On the way up the stairs to bed, I heard Amy say to her mom, "Mom, me and Dad are bonding!"

Bonding, as Amy put it, is connecting with our children in a consistent, deep, and committed way. Bonding is very important to our children's overall development and sense of well-being. If you look at the plot of the Bible, the main story line is God's desire and attempts to bond with us. He not only wants to bond us to him, but he also wants us to bond with each other.

When Nancie and I married, we began to experience a oneness that transcended physical union. It was a deep spiritual connection. The nucleus of our family began. When our children were delivered into our relationship, something even greater happened. We both felt what millions of parents feel— a compelling need to nurture, protect, love, and provide for our young.

At the moment of our children's birth, it did not matter to me whether they were boys or girls, cute or ugly. As each child entered our lives, we felt the awesome truth: This child—the combined genetics of our union, flesh of our flesh and bone of our bone—is wholly ours. We were ecstatic! To experience this is one of life's great moments of joy. A similar thing happened, just as powerful and just as joyful, when we adopted Amy.

But initial bonding is only the beginning of connection. Over time, we develop a sort of sixth sense about our loved ones. We know their dispositions. We learn their likes and dislikes. We discover the things that please them and the hot buttons that set them off. We can tell by looking at them when something is wrong. We become loyal, protective, tolerant, loving, and deeply attached. And as a family we develop strong and unique problem-solving abilities.[1]

Connection comes from shared experience. People who have gone through a hostage situation together bond in unique ways. People who have fought in wars together bond in special ways. College roommates often bond. Childhood friends sometimes bond for life. Accident victims will bond with the medical team that gave them CPR. Shared experience connects people in powerful ways. It is never more powerful than with family.

People who have never bonded tend to become deeply disturbed later in life. This is the tragedy of some children, like Joe, who are caught in the web of the foster-care system. Joe is an eight-year-old who was passed from place to place. When he was two, he was ripped from a loving home that had planned to adopt him. But a court order gave him back to his father, a convicted felon who had served jail time for burglary and theft.

But after gaining custody of his son, Joe's father died, leaving Joe to his second wife. This woman soon moved in with another man, who had done jail time for criminal sexual abuse. Before long, school officials were saying that Joe was suicidal—"a danger to himself and others."

Joe's case came back to the courts only because of a state's attorney who said that Joe, at the age of eight, had committed aggravated criminal sexual assault. Joe has never again seen the family who had wanted to adopt him six years ago, a stable couple who had given Joe the love connection he so desperately needed for the first two years of his life.

Sadly, Joe's case is not unique. Just today I read in the newspaper about four-year-old Richard, who was taken from his adoptive home, put into a van, and driven away. Promises were made by the biological parent that Richard's adoptive parents would be able to visit him regularly. A year has now gone by, and Richard has not seen or spoken to the ones he loved and was bonded to.

Knowledgeable authorities in the field of children's

health and development, from the American Academy of Pediatrics to the director of the various state divisions of the Department of Children's and Family Services, agree that to remove children so abruptly from everything and everyone they have ever loved and to refuse to permit them any contact with those people does great damage. Yet it still happens nearly every day in our confused and bewildered legal system.[2]

Dr. Lewis Smedes says the connection process helps people feel "owned." He believes that children who feel owned can go on to make fundamental discoveries about themselves: "I am someone who has been loved from the beginning; . . . I am someone to whom someone else made an unconditional commitment; . . . I am someone whose parents consider me worthy of the love they give; I have the power to own myself; I take responsibility for my life, I am proud to be who I am, and I have joy in being myself." Feeling owned, says Smedes, is love's way to immunize children against shame.[3]

The concept of connection is an awesome one, awesome because it is at the root of who we are and who we become. We don't choose our family. The obligations our parents take on to love and provide for us are not contractual in nature. Family ties are not voluntary. You can choose your friends, but you cannot choose your family. Your sister is your sister whether you like it or not. The family connection is core to you. Everything we know about family connection suggests that the strong connections between parent and child are the keys to raising emotionally and spiritually healthy children. Bonding is an essential part of having good ground in your home.

🌿 Communicating with Those We Love

In the all-important world of family relations, three words are almost as powerful as the famous "I love you." They are, "Maybe you're right."

OREN ARNOLD

THE FIRST time I met Nancie's family was when I drove her home from college at the beginning of summer. I had just graduated, and she had finished her first year. We had fallen in love during that year, and I had proposed to her. I later had asked her father, over the phone, for his permission to marry his beloved daughter.

I will never forget the night Nancie and I crowded together in a phone booth on the college campus in southern California. She dialed the number, a collect call to Montana, and said, "Hi, Daddy. This is Nancie. Bill is here with me, and he has something he wants to ask." My knees were shaking, my heart pounding. How would he react? What should I say?

For days I had gone over my speech. I had rehearsed long dissertations on love, commitment, maturity, the future, my ability to earn a living, timing, my family background, and any other subject I thought he might quiz me about. The fact that Nancie's father and I had never met put both of us at a distinct disadvantage. "Mr. Pearson," I said, "Nancie and I have decided that we want to be married to each other. I know you have never met me, but I was wondering if you would give your permission for us to announce our engagement at the junior-senior banquet next week?"

Silence. Dead silence.

It seemed like an eternity.

Then, in a soft voice, he said, "Well, I s'pose that'd be all right."

That was it. No questions, no quizzing, no sermons, no stipulations—nothing else. After a few more seconds of silence, I said, "Thank you, Mr. Pearson. I look forward to meeting you. Here's Nancie."

Gunder Pearson was a man of few words, Nancie had assured me.

He became my father-in-law, and during the twelve years we had together before he died, we became good friends. But I learned that Nancie was right. He was a man of few words. His most complimentary comments after a delicious meal Nancie's mom had prepared would be a quiet, "Not bad." That was it. And if you missed it, it was rarely, if ever, repeated.

Gunder Pearson, the consummate farmer, a man of the soil, at one with his land and his God. And if you worked at it, he would connect with you too. But building bridges with words was not his forte. And yet this deep and simple man was a dynamic force in hundreds of lives, especially the down-and-outers. Having lost his parents at an early age in North Dakota and having brought his younger brothers and sisters with him to homestead in Montana had given Gunder compassion. He told me of times he and his siblings had nothing more than a few withered potatoes to eat, and the shack all seven of them lived in was no bigger than a small bedroom. Hard times had given him a heart bigger than the heart of any other person I had ever met.

But hard times had also smothered the words inside of him. His father's death when Gunder was a small child, his stepfather's suicide, and then his mother's death—all before Gunder had lived for eighteen years—had pounded the words and grief back down inside him like a concrete cap on a gushing oil well. The way to deal with disaster and hardship in those depression days was to swallow it and go on. They knew no other choices if they wanted to survive.

It is easy to see this now, in retrospect. But at the time of our phone call from California to Montana to ask for his permission to marry, it was not so easy for Nancie to see. When we hung up the phone, Nancie began to feel that her father's lack of comment or probing meant he did not care enough to confront or question.

He cared all right, maybe more deeply than most fathers. But he could not bring himself to speak. Nancie's mother, Harriet, always said that Nancie was the "apple of her daddy's eye." His feelings at the moment were just too big and too deep. I sometimes wonder if he thought that if he spoke with even a tiny crack of emotion, the entire dam would break.

I recall many different times when he spoke to me with pride about one of his three sons, but I never heard him say those same things directly to them. It was as if the feelings were too awesome, too potentially explosive, ever to say to the object of one's affection. Like Moses viewing the glory of God, one could take seeing only the afterglow; a direct glance would kill you. So Gunder could speak life-giving words of pride and confidence to a son-in-law about his children, but he could rarely say the words to his children themselves.

Nancie told me that Gunder's children all knew he was very proud of them. They knew because he bragged about them to others all the time. He went out of his way to introduce his children to others. He was so proud that it became a standing family joke: "Daddy introduces us to everyone he meets!" But he just wasn't able to verbalize the deep feelings of love and joy he felt for his children.

I suspect that there are a lot of Gunders out there who, for whatever reason, find it very difficult to make a good verbal connection. We fathers can preach, admonish, give orders, even shout if needed. But when we try to connect with healing words of love, with complimentary words of encouragement, and with attitudes of empathetic listening, we often choke. We are the leaders, the providers, the authoritarians, the in-your-face coaches, but we are not very good nurturers. Some fathers continue to pass down the "manly" ideas of how to relate—historically not a nurture-type model. Some men in our culture are not very good at being open and attentive. We are still learning how to be vulnerable.

Therman Munson, one of the great catchers for the New York Yankees, once said of his father, "When I started to play in organized games, I could go four for four, and he'd get all over me for some fielding lapse. To friends and neighbors, he'd always be building me up, but it was sure tough to drag a compliment out of him directly."[4] Bob Keeshan, who played television's Captain Kangaroo, once told of a time he was helping his father in the garden. After Keeshan had pulled up a scrawny piece of brush by the roots, he heard his father whisper with pride to the neighbor, "Strong as a bull, that boy. He's wonderful." Bob went on to say, "I never let my father know that I had heard, and he never let me know how he felt about my childhood achievements. Admiration had to be expressed discreetly, and if I had caught him, he'd have been embarrassed. Too bad. I could have used some confidence-building from time to time."[5]

Communication does not just happen. Like a garden, it needs cultivation, water, and sunshine. It needs our attention, and it takes time and nurturing. Communication is not just getting our message across. It involves the *way* we express ourselves to our children. Children want to have good communication with their parents. One woman told me, "My dad wrote me one letter, and that was over twenty years ago when I was in the Air Force basic training. It is one of my most treasured possessions, especially because my dad never, ever writes anything. How great to have my father's written, tangible expression of love!"

Meaningful communication involves the art of listening, the feeling of being heard and understood. This is a problem my children had with me while they were growing up. I have good communication skills when it comes to giving sermons and speeches. I only wish my listening and empathy skills were half as good. I can debate, make a point, drive it home, pound it into the ground, dazzle you with facts, bury you with clever words and arguments. But to *hear* with my heart—that's a skill I have to work at very hard.

Listening is an art. It is one of the most wonderful gifts you can give to another person. It is also quite rare. Most of us listen only because we need the time to think of our next response. We are not really listening with our hearts and *hearing* what the other person is saying.

As one teenager said of his father, "Do you know what I am? I'm a comma."

"What do you mean?" the listener replied.

"Well, whenever I talk to my dad, he stops talking and makes a 'comma.' But when I'm finished, he starts right up again as if I hadn't said a thing. I'm just a comma in the middle of his speeches."[6]

One night when Andy was a senior in high school, he was sprawled out on the living-room floor. We marveled at how this kid grew. What on earth was in his head? So Nancie, as her mother had asked her, asked, "Andy, what does it feel like to be you?"

He said, "You have no idea! I don't think you even know who I am."

"Try me," she said. They had a great conversation, ending up with his telling her how much he missed his older brother Chris, with whom he'd shared a bedroom all his life until Chris went away to college. And he told her about being lonely, about some dreams and plans he had. He allowed Nancie to have just a little peek at what was in his heart. It was just a crack, but it was beautiful!

Many children have a hard time with words. It can be intimidating to speak to an adult when your word skills don't match theirs. If we parents are not careful, we can make it more difficult for our children to open up by using our superior verbal skills. When children feel they cannot verbally compete, it makes them reluctant to attempt to get their own point across. Eventually it could cause them to avoid asking, avoid sharing, avoid trying to seek clarification, and certainly avoid trying to change a parent's mind. If we don't listen, we will soon find out we have a house full of children who don't listen either.

Of all the sins I have committed as a parent, I grieve more over my lack of sensitivity in this area than probably any other. I was busy getting my point across, trying to mold and shape character with the power of words rather than tune into my children's heartfelt needs and learn the art of reading between the lines. There were times when I was not very approachable. David Augsburger said, "A child can be the object of much affection and still not feel loved. . . . Feeling loved and being heard are so similar, it's difficult to distinguish between the two."[7]

Not all was lost, mind you. As my children grew, two things happened. First, I became increasingly aware that my communication skills needed to change. Nancie has been a huge help in this area, and so has our daughter, Amy. Second, our children never doubted my intense love for them, and as their own communication skills improved, they were willing to risk talking back to me. Today, most of them can tell their father not only what they are feeling but also where to get off when the "old speech giver" fires up another sermon.

Some of my children are better at verbal expression than others. One of my sons just has a hard time getting out what's inside. He will call me on the phone, and I know he has something important he wants to say, but it will take him forever to get it out. "Well, Dad . . . I . . . well . . . I went to get my car fixed and . . . well . . . you know . . . I mean . . . well, this guy said . . . oh, man, I don't know if he's telling me the truth, you know. . . . I mean . . . the mechanic said that the transmission is . . . well . . . he thinks that if he fixes it . . . I mean . . . well, to fix it will cost about as much as to replace it . . . but . . . you know, I mean. . . ."

By now I know the gist of what he is saying because I have been through this before. My son is saying, "My car broke down; it's the transmission; it is going to cost a lot to fix it or replace it; I think I may need to get another estimate to make sure I'm not being ripped off; I need you to loan me some money." I will usually listen for a while, and when it is appropriate, I will ask some clarifying questions like "Did you get a written estimate of the cost?" and "Do you need me to loan you some money to get you through this situation?"

I will also add comments of empathy. "I bet this really bummed you out, having a major breakdown like that. I remember when I had a major repair and cash was short. It kind of made me sick and frustrated all at the same time. I'll help you as much as I can." This usually helps and lets my son feel heard and understood.

Paul Tournier says, "It is impossible to overemphasize the immense need humans have to be really listened to, to be taken seriously, to be understood. No one can develop freely in this world and find a full life without feeling understood by at least one person. . . . Listen to all the conversations of our world, between nations as well as those between couples. They are for the most part dialogues of the deaf."[8] Tournier goes on to say, "Deep down inside [a child's] inner wells are a multitude of needs, questions, hurts, and longings. Like a tiny bucket, their tongues splash out these things. The busy, insensitive, preoccupied parent, steamrollering through the day, misses many a cue and sails right past choice moments never to be repeated or retrieved."[9]

We parents tend to get so caught up in teaching our children about life that we forget the special importance of *communicating* with them. Someone has said, "Communion is giving and receiving; preaching is all give." Too often we are talking *at* our children, talking *through* our children, or talking *over* our children. Stephen Covey says that "most people do not really listen with the intent to understand; rather, they listen with the intent to reply."[10]

When our children try to talk to us, we must learn to get down on one knee, face-to-face, and try to get into their world, into their hearts. When our children say, "Hey, Mom," we may need to stop and pay attention, make eye contact, focus, and listen. It may not take much, but the attention given will affirm our children in powerful ways.

To be understood and affirmed. To be taken seriously. To have someone at home show keen interest in my life, trials, and triumphs. To be noticed, not talked over, but really heard—this is communication.

🌿 Becoming an Approachable Parent

When we're available to our children, it says,
"You are important."
And when we're not available it says,
"Oh, yes, I love you, but other things still come ahead of you.
You are not really that important."
JOSH MCDOWELL

ONCE, when Nancie and I were leaving to go on a speaking engagement, our daughter, Amy, six years old at the time, began acting strangely. The evening before Nancie and I were to leave, Amy began jumping up and down on our bed, deliberately messing up things that Nancie had laid out to put in the luggage. Nancie scolded Amy and told her to stop. When Amy came to the kitchen for dinner, she grabbed her place setting off the table and put it back on the counter. Her face was a storm cloud. Nancie realized something deep was troubling her.

Nancie got down on the floor where Amy was sitting and took her in her arms. Nancie looked into her eyes and softly said, "Amy, what's wrong?"

Amy threw her arms around Nancie and burst into sobs. "Don't leave me, Mommy! Please don't leave me. I feel bad when you're not here."

Nancie's heart broke as she watched the pain pour out of this child who had been abandoned on a doorstep in South Korea and placed in an orphanage until she was three years old. Nancie sat there on the floor and wept with Amy, knowing that abandoned children have big holes in their hearts. Nancie wondered, *How should I parent this little girl with this big problem?* She felt overwhelmed with feelings of inadequacy and helplessness.

Suddenly Amy stopped sniffling and looked at Nancie, surprised. "Hey—why are you crying, Mommy?" she said.

"Amy, I feel sad because you're upset," Nancie replied. "But I promise you I will come back. I will never stop being your mother. I love you always."

Amy grinned. "Oh, thank you, Mommy! I love you too." She kissed Nancie exuberantly and was once again all smiles. Amy was visibly relieved to see that Nancie cared and identified with her feelings. Moments like that are healing moments in children's lives. This incident could have ended in a spanking or some other disciplinary action, but if it had, this healing moment would have been lost.

When we are preoccupied or intensely involved in our

own agenda, it is easy for our family members to read us as unapproachable. The body language at these times says, "I don't have time for you now." It may come while you are reading the paper, watching television, or doing a household chore. We are a busy people, a fast moving culture, a get-ahead-and-succeed society, a find-yourself generation. In this environment, while we do things for our children in a frantic load-the-van-and-go mode, we often unknowingly send signals that tell our spouses and our children that we have no time to be approached, no time to listen to their lives. The schedule is so tight, the agenda so full, that we have no time for interruptions.

Being approachable is not an issue of time; it is an issue of attitude. When we are sensitive and perceptive in reading other family members' signals, it may only take a concerned "How are you doing, honey?" comment and a hug to place another family member back on track. When we are approachable, it means the connection channels are open, the phone line is not giving a busy signal.

Approachability also involves good feedback to others in our family. It may mean asking clarifying or even confrontational questions like "You seem a little down today. Are you feeling okay?" or "You're awfully quiet. Would you like to talk with me?" Approachability opens the door for telling the truth and being able to confront in constructive ways.[11]

When we adopted our daughter, Amy, I sensed at the time that the adjustment would be greatest for our youngest son, Andy. He was seven years old and was used to being center stage, like most youngest siblings. Obviously, when Amy first joined our family, she was getting lots of attention. Nancie and I were intent on giving her a solid start in our family, and our "needs antennae" were aimed squarely at her. Andy was also being displaced as the youngest child. One day I said to him, "Andy, sometimes we can feel as if we are not getting enough attention. If you ever feel that way, I want you to come to me and say, 'I need some attention.'"

Less than a day later, Andy came to me and said, "Dad, I need some attention." I took some time to be alone with him and give him my undivided attention. By being approachable, I was able to help Andy through this tough adjustment process.

More often, however, I have found that my own lack of ability to be approachable is connected to my focus on my own agenda. I was building a publishing business while my kids were growing up. Nancie and I were both intensely involved in this process. We not only went to work at the office every day, but we often brought our work home with us.

One of the magazines we published was *Virtue,* a Christian magazine for women. When Andy was young, he could not pronounce *Virtue.* He would always say, "Birchyou." One evening at the dinner table, while Nancie and I were continuing to drag that day's work into the conversation between us, Andy piped up and said, "Birchyou, Birchyou, Birchyou. All I ever hear around here is Birchyou, Birchyou, Birchyou!" We all cracked up laughing, but it was a good indicator of the signals we were sending our children.

Unless you are an approachable parent, you will not know whether your children are testing you to see how far they can push you or if they are simply trying to get you to connect with them. Sometimes parents who send signals of being unapproachable will mistake children's "acting out" as a discipline problem rather than a parent problem. If you assess your own approachability quotient, you may discover that all your children really want is some attention from you.

We have all heard the songs and poems about dads and moms who did not have time to romp with their kids while they were growing up, and most of us have sharp pangs of guilt about those times we have been unavailable. Being approachable is a choice we make. It will often require sacrifice on our part. Sometimes it means sacrificing things as insignificant as the evening paper or a favorite television show. Sometimes it might mean telling a valued client that the meeting will have to wait until tomorrow. More often, it just means being attentive to the signals and responsive to the needs. Approachability is a vital part of connecting with your family, an essential habit of a healthy home.

✍ Connecting through Togetherness

No one who reaches the end of life has ever looked back and said,
"Oh, I wish I had spent more time at the office instead of with my kids."
BARBARA BUSH

EVER since our children were very small, I have been taking photographs. I like to take slides and put them in slide carousels. Each carousel of about one hundred and forty slides represents one year of our life together. I start with a photo taken on New Year's Day and proceed through the kids' basketball season, on to Easter, sometimes a graduation, through some birthdays, summer vacations and fishing trips, more birthdays, Thanksgiving, and finally Christmas. Some years there are extra carousels, like the year we saved up our money and frequent-flyer awards and took the entire family to the Cayman Islands.

Many of our pictures are taken in the San Juan Islands on our boat. It is a favorite vacation spot with unlimited islands to explore, bald eagles, dolphins, and killer whales fishing for their daily catch. Our little cabin cruiser will sleep all of us if we snuggle up.

At night we tell each other stories and listen to tapes of Garrison Keillor talking about Lake Wobegon. We laugh and reminisce. Sometimes our group consists of just our immediate family, and sometimes Grandpa Carmichael has been with me and my children on a fishing trip. Grandpa is a great story-teller, and the kids are always mesmerized by his tales. There have been many magic moments on that boat, and our children often speak of the times we have had there. On many occasions we have had the opportunity to discuss matters of deep significance—spiritual issues, character issues, life decisions—while on the *Red Dolphin*.

In those slide carousels are pictures of us in a rented motor home, crammed together, listening to the rain pelt the metal top. There are pictures of us playing games together near Glacier Park, Montana, in an old cabin that Nancie's father built. There are pictures of us hiking up a local mountain to pick huckleberries. There are pictures of our kids playing basketball, from grade school through college. Nancie and I figured out one day that we have sat in the bleachers for over seven hundred basketball games, watching our kids and yelling at referees.

It is interesting to view our lives in a yearly slide show. There are a few years when the carousels are only partially full. Not even all the birthdays were photographed in some years. In thinking back on those years, I realize those were years I was preoccupied with other things. One of those years was the year we made the decision to sell our publishing company to another larger company. It was an exhausting year of commuting to Chicago and back, reorganizing, doing financial projections, and gearing up for new growth and marketing. The photo carousel reveals that we didn't take much of a vacation that year.

In some early years, I worked for a mission organization and traveled overseas. These are sparse photo years too. I would be gone for four or five weeks at a time, home for a week or two, and then gone again. During those years I took hundreds of pictures of cute little children from Africa, India, and Samoa, but I didn't take many of my own children. I did not have much time for family in those years, and the photo carousels prove it.

The pursuit of some of those things was burning brightly for me at those times. I thought of them as the most important things I could and should be doing. And they were important. I helped to build a strong magazine-publishing ministry. I helped build schools and churches in Third World countries. And I had the chance to minister to thousands of people. But now as I look back, nothing I did has more significance, more satisfaction, or even more eternal investment than the moments spent together with my wife and children.

Quality moments are not setups. We don't just say, "Let's have a quality moment," and then have one. Quality moments with family happen spontaneously. They are dispersed between hours and days of routine. Of the hundreds of hours we have spent on our boat, most of them were spent routinely fixing meals, cleaning the boat, telling kids to stop bickering or to stop throwing rocks at the seagulls, untangling fishing lines, and looking for things we had misplaced. They also included riding in our truck with the boat hooked on behind, listening to kids whine about being bored and tired.

Holidays are hard work, especially for Nancie. Every Christmas she invests her time and energy baking cookies, decorating the house, buying and wrapping gifts, and fixing gourmet meals. She admits it's not much fun doing all those things and then falling into bed exhausted at night. The tension can run pretty high during these times. Kids look to these times as fun, but any parent knows that creating special times together is a lot of work.

Quality moments are the result of spending lots of time together. Have you ever been fishing? How much time is spent with your limp line in the water, bobbing, casting, or trolling for the fish? Most of it. Good fisherman spend hours waiting for the fish to bite, waiting for the object of their trip to swallow their bait. If a fisherman said, "I don't have very much time to spend fishing, but what little time I do have is quality time," you can bet he would not catch very many fish. The same is true with time together as a family. Most of togetherness is routine stuff, but it is out of that routine time that memorable togetherness is built.

Togetherness includes the very real parts of daily living: working, playing, eating meals, riding in cars, basketball and soccer games, band concerts, watching videos, parent-teacher conferences, eating out, sleepovers, attending church, praying together.

A survey asked fifteen hundred children, "What do you think makes for a happy family?" They did not list fancy houses, more money, new cars, or other status symbols. "Doing things together" was their response. What families do is not nearly as important as the fact that they do it together.[12] And it isn't just the fun stuff. Doing daily chores like housecleaning and yard work should be a big part of togetherness.

I love the story of the emperor penguins in Antarctica. Scientists tell us that if they don't stay together, they die. They huddle together by the thousands, supplying each other enough warmth to survive the brutal subzero weather during the winter months. It is said that they take turns moving to the outside of the pack while those in the middle sleep and stay warm. For them, togetherness means survival.

A family is *we* rather than *I*. A brother and sister in central Oregon have been an inspiration to all of us. These two children became orphans as teenagers when their mother died of diabetes and then, less than a year later, their father suddenly died of complications from hepatitis C. Many friends and neighbors surrounded these children with love and prayers. Some of the teenagers' first words after the deaths were, "We are going to stay together. We know we can make it." And they have. The sister works after school in order to help provide for her brother. They are totally committed to each other and the preservation of what is left of their family. They have had options to split up and go live with relatives, but they have chosen to stay together.

As Christian counselor Dr. Paul Pearsall said, "Our most basic instinct is not for survival, but for family. Most of us would give our own life for the survival of a family member. . . . Such a group is the basic building block of our world, the place where the miracle of 'us' takes place."[13]

Today we struggle with the togetherness issue because so many voices scream for our time and attention. And this is especially true at the stage of life when our children are young. It is what Nancie calls "the gathering years." We are gathering up our education and work experience, trying to put them into some type of meaningful careers; we are gathering up a family by having babies; we are gathering friends; we are gathering assets like homes, cars, and investment portfolios; and we are even gathering up our teachings, spiritual insights, and philosophies of life, trying to make sense of them and match them with our goals. And with all of these, we are gathering up new responsibilities, worries, challenges, and concerns.

It is no wonder that most young parents feel family time competes with so many other things that seem to demand attention. In this time pressure cooker, many parents end up missing out on their children's childhoods.

Being absent while your kids are growing up does not happen just to those who divorce. Parents can be right in the same room with their children and let the opportunity for connection slide because they are preoccupied with other things.

This is especially true of many fathers. Statistics tell us that while the amount of time fathers spend in daily meaningful interaction with their children is going up, from less than five minutes per day a few years ago, it is still not enough.

One report indicates that the three things fathers say most often to their children are, "I'm too tired," "We don't have enough money," and "Keep quiet!"[14]

Raising our children is a special calling—you would not be reading this book if you did not agree. What is more difficult to realize is how important the stage you are in *now* may be. There are critical moments that will come only once in a child's development. There may only be one window of opportunity when a child will ask a certain question or one time when a teenager will be open to your input. If we miss that moment, it may be gone forever. Time is a nonrenewable resource, and when it's gone, it's forever gone.

I know this is true. I can remember back to the days when my children were out on the lush grassy fields I am viewing out my window as I write this. They would be playing touch football and Wiffle ball, and they frequently asked me to join in. Many times I said yes; many times I said no. And yet, I do not wish for one single yes back to trade for doing something else, but looking out there at that empty field makes me wish I could have every no back and trade it for another yes.

Togetherness means wasting time and doing nonsense. That may be a crude way to put it, but often our togetherness as a family carries with it little immediate meaning for the parent when compared to finishing up a big contract at the office, paying the monthly bills, cleaning the house, shopping for a new car, or watching a sports spectacular on television. Idle time with our kids, *at the time,* can be boring or nerve-wracking. Listening to their bickering, getting down on their level with foolish nonsensical giggles, wiping runny noses, and washing dirty little hands can seem like a waste of our precious time.

For some of you, this decision about spending time with your children comes naturally and easily. But many of us struggle with the allotment of time demanded by a variety of priorities. Things just don't always go as planned, so we have to make choices about how we spend our time. If young parents can get perspective on this issue (which is very hard for young parents to do, considering the other demands and attractions out there), they will see that the investment of time with their children now will pay huge dividends later in life.

It doesn't have to be a big deal or an expensive event—an evening at home with some games, a bedtime story, a walk in the park, doing some chores together, a few minutes playing catch or shooting hoops is usually enough—especially if it is done often. It offers you a chance to connect, to be intimate, to say words of encouragement, to pass on family values, to build your children's self-confidence, to listen to their concerns.

Your children need to feel they have you completely and exclusively once in a while. They need to sense by your actions that they are the most important person in the world to you. This is not something we give our children as an option. It is vital to their healthy development and their sense of self-worth.[15]

Words will not substitute for focused attention. Some parents make continual verbalizations of their love for their children. But "I love you" or "You matter to me" are shallow words if they are not accompanied by your time and attention. Certainly your kids will accept these words—all children will cling to what they can get—but in the end, these children will end up not feeling valued by their parents.[16]

Little children's lives don't wait for us to get through with doing our thing. Growth cannot be put off for another day when we have more time. Life is always urgent, without any possibility of postponement. Once our children are born, their lives are fired at us point-blank.

✎ Connecting through Touch
A kiss from my mother made me a painter.
BENJAMIN WEST

ONE OF our grown sons came to visit us this week. When he left this morning, he kissed me on the cheek as he has done since he was a child. Some fathers find it difficult to show affection to their sons. To them, hugging or kissing is not a manly thing to do. We men have been so culturally programmed that some of us feel it is appropriate to hug only if the person we are hugging is our father and at least one of us has a terminal disease; only if we are performing the Heimlich maneuver on a person who's choking; or only if we're a professional athlete and a teammate has just hit a home run or scored a touchdown!

Appropriate touch is an important way of connecting. Several studies have shown that infants who are touched, cuddled, and held sleep better, gain necessary weight better, and are healthier than babies who are not touched by a loving caregiver. Loving touch communicates security and builds children's self-esteem.

Obviously, we are speaking here of healthy, nonsexual

touching. A hug or kiss, a pat on the back, an arm across a shoulder, holding hands, stroking one's hair are all ways to say, "I care deeply about you." This kind of touching imparts healing. As writer and theologian Donald Joy said, "'Hold me tight!' is the persistent human cry."[17]

Nancie recalls one day when Amy came off the bus in tears. Amy is very nearsighted, and a boy had teased her about her thick glasses, calling her Four Eyes. Trying to soothe Amy, Nancie said, "Oh, Amy, he didn't mean anything. Don't worry about it."

A few minutes later, Nancie realized that Amy was upstairs, still crying. Amy really was hurt, and Nancie's comment had in essence told her, "You don't have a right to be hurt. You don't have a right to feel pain over this." When Nancie realized this, she ran upstairs, held Amy, stroked her cheeks, and listened to her pain. After a few minutes of hugging, Amy's sobs subsided, and she was able to let go of the hurt.

Hugging is like a miracle drug. It helps reduce stress, assists the body's immune system, and induces sleep. It makes us feel loved and cared for. Hugging melts hostilities and fosters closeness. It is a vital part of connection and togetherness.

One of our favorite theologians, Winnie the Pooh, was walking down the road one day when Piglet sidled up to him from behind. "'Pooh!' he whispered.

'Yes, Piglet?'

'Nothing,' said Piglet, taking Pooh's paw. 'I just wanted to be sure of you.'"

Appropriate touching helps us to be sure of each other. It bonds us together in deep connection.

✒ Connecting through Commitment

When states instituted no-fault divorce,
they decided by and large
that wanderlust would be a state-protected emotion,
while loyalty was on its own.

MAGGIE GALLAHER

AN IMPORTANT way we can build a sense of connection for our children is through our commitment to our spouse. A solid marriage provides one of the deepest foundational connections our children will know.

From the outside, Nancie and I thought Ralph and Laurie had a great marriage. It was obvious they both adored their children, and in the ten years we had known them, they gave no hint that they were anything less than happy.

But then it happened. Laurie announced that she was bored. She had gone to work for Ted in the local bookstore, trying to find something more exciting to do than driving her kids to Little League and attending school concerts. Ted seemed so much more alive and charming to Laurie than her husband did. Ralph was not as attentive to their marriage as he could have been. Although he was a good father to fourteen-year-old Cindy and eleven-year-old Paul, he was spending a lot of time building his new business.

We live in a small town that boasts a population of 850, so it was a shock to the entire community when Laurie announced that she was divorcing Ralph to marry Ted. She and Ted had been having an affair for several weeks. Ted was dissatisfied with his marriage too.

Just like that, two sets of vows went up in smoke. Two

other spouses became victims, and five children became the unwilling pawns in the battle for custody.

Against his will, Paul, a friend of one of our sons, was uprooted at the age of eleven. Paul lost not only his roots but also the good ground of home. He was bounced from parent to parent. I've followed Paul's emotional struggles over the years, and now, at age twenty-six, Paul still seems lost. He has drifted from college to college and job to job, a nomadic victim of the crushing destruction of his base of support and source of nurture.

The fact is, one of the greatest destroyers of children's sense of connection is divorce. As professor Allan Bloom said, "To children, the voluntary separation of parents seems worse than their death precisely because it is voluntary."[18]

Children instinctively believe they have a right to the attention and nurturing of both of their parents. Family was supposed to be the one sure thing for children, no matter what. When divorce occurs, children are forced to face the awful truth that the two people they rely on to nurture them no longer wish to nurture each other. These children can never resolve or settle the issue. Their parents' decision to divorce will shape the children's lives in powerful ways, yet the children have no say.

Divorce destroys children's sense of belonging. It breaks the connection, fractures the bonding, and forces children to do some "unlinking" that screams against everything they know about connection. They lose faith with the idea that some connections are permanent bonds.

To ensure our children's sense of connection and belonging, we must remember that the stability of our marriage relationship affects our children for their entire lives. Good marriages take hard work. Good marriages are not something we "get" by saying "I do." Good marriages are something we do. It is a matter of the heart. It is understanding the meaning of commitment. Working hard to create love and harmony is a choice we must make every day if we want our children to have a sense of connection and wholeness.

Connecting through Grace
If you judge people, you have no time to love them.
MOTHER TERESA

ALL OF our children love to play basketball. Several of them have been blessed with college scholarships. When our children were younger, Nancie and I tried to use basketball to motivate them to get good grades in school. The school's eligibility rule was that team members had to have a passing grade in every class; that meant Ds or better. But our family rule was that our children needed a C or better in every class in order to have our permission to play on the team.

Our son Eric and I have a vivid memory about this rule. The entire family agrees that Eric may have the most raw talent of any of our children. In high school he was lauded as one of the state's best players and was selected to the state's all-star team. He went on to have an excellent college basketball career. But back in eighth grade it almost came to an end, except for grace.

I said that Eric had the most natural ability, but his study habits did not always match his ability. When the preliminary grade report came out, it indicated that Eric was getting a D in two subjects. I reminded him that these had to come up before basketball season started.

Practice for the season began, and shortly thereafter the grades came out. Eric had brought one of the Ds up to a C+, but the other one remained a D. I felt sick to my stomach when I saw the grade. We all knew what it meant for Eric. I wanted him to play; I think I enjoyed the games almost as much as he did. But I decided I had to stick with our rule.

Eric was lying on his bed when I walked into his room. He was a gangly kid of fourteen, with braces on his teeth and legs so long he looked like a praying mantis. He sat up when I came in the room. "Eric," I said with that somber tone that meant something was very wrong, "did you see your report card that came today?"

"Yes," he whispered.

"Well, Son, I hate more than anything to do this, but I am afraid you will not be able to play basketball since that was the rule we both knew and agreed to."

He looked up at me with tears in his eyes and said, "I really tried to bring that grade up, Dad. Please give me one more chance. I promise I will work hard and get it up."

"There's no time to bring it up before the season starts. You knew the rule, and you should have worked harder than you did," I stated matter-of-factly as I began to leave the room. "I'll call the coach and let him know."

As I left the room, I brushed past Nancie, who had quietly slipped in. Eric burst into gut-wrenching sobs. I felt sicker. I went to my room feeling as if I had just been the one to pull the switch on the electric chair.

If anyone has the ministry of mercy, it is Nancie. She was

left there in his room to do the comforting for the decision I had made. Several minutes went by. As I paced up and down in my bedroom, I kept thinking and wishing there were options to my actions and decision. As I prayed quietly, the Lord reminded me of a time when I was a boy and begged for another chance.

Like Eric, I did not get very good grades. But my parents did not have athletics to hang over my head, since I played very little. But I remembered once, when I was about twelve years old, being invited to go skiing with some friends. My mother tried to use this as an incentive to get me to study for an upcoming test. She said, "If you do not do well on that test, you cannot go skiing this weekend." I studied as hard as I knew how. My sister, who was an honor student, helped me study, and I thought I was prepared. But when I took the test, the teacher seemed to ask all the questions I had not asked myself. I did better than I normally would have done, but I still got a D. I begged my mother to let me go anyway. I pleaded for mercy, but she would not budge. "You knew the rule," she said. I recalled that those were the very words I had just uttered to Eric.

Nancie left Eric and came into our bedroom. "Bill, is there some other way to handle this?" she asked. "I feel that we are at a real crossroads here and a little mercy may be in order," she said.

I knew she was right, but what should I do? I wanted to be consistent in my discipline—this was the rule. No one would fault me for sticking to my guns on this. But something deep inside me said that Eric should be given another chance.

I went back up to Eric's room. I found him with his head

buried in his pillow. I lay down beside him on the bed and put my arms around him. "Eric, somehow I think that God wants me to take another look at this situation," I said. "Would you sign a contract that guarantees you will make the effort to bring these grades up by the next report period if I agree to let you play ball?"

Before I could think, long skinny arms grabbed my neck. I felt his warm wet tears as he kissed my neck. "Dad, I promise I will. Thanks for giving me another chance," he choked out.

And he did. Every year Eric and I renewed that agreement, and it held all the way through school. Basketball not only paid for most of Eric's college education, but it was the source of keeping him motivated to get acceptable grades.

Sometimes a little grace at the right time will not only strengthen the connection between you and your child but also point a life in the right direction forever. Who knows how far afield Eric would have gone or what bitterness might have set in if basketball had been taken away from him at that juncture? Who knows how the connective relationship might have been damaged without his mother's sensitivity? Grace was in order then, and it has often been in order since then.

As pastor Walter Wangerin says in his book *As for Me and My House*, "Forgiveness is a Divine absurdity. For-give-ness is a holy, complete, unqualified giving." And we must remember that it is better to bind our children to us through acts of mercy and grace than it is through acts of fear and punishment.

Mending is a good analogy for what families need to do for each other. We are each a part of the fabric of those we love, and it's a good idea to do some daily repairs for hurts, appre-

hensions, and wounds inflicted on those we love. Forgiveness
lubricates friction. Someone said, "Forgiveness is celestial
amnesia." It doesn't matter how strong we are; all of us need
care and mending sometimes. It takes many acts of grace,
many reaffirmations, and many gestures of love to hold us
together as we journey through life.

Don't be afraid to ask for grace. When you make a mistake, ask your family for some grace. Some parents feel it is a
sign of weakness to repent and ask for forgiveness, when in reality it is a sign of strength. How else can your children learn
about grace and repentance if they don't see you dip into its
solace once in a while? Your acts of repentance will bond and
connect your children to you in a powerful way and put a
needed nutrient into the good ground of your home.

✍ Threats to Connection

Because we have come to take the unnecessary to be
necessary, we have lost all sense of necessity, either natural or
cultural.
ALLAN BLOOM

THE MOST conspicuous threat to family togetherness is
found in nearly every family room: the television. In some
homes, it has turned the family from a close-knit unit into a
disjointed collection of individuals. In a majority of homes,
television isn't just another option for entertainment; it is
the central feature of attention. As critic Kenneth Myers has
observed, "Television can no longer be considered simply a
part of the culture; rather it is our culture. Television is the

single most significant shared reality in our entire society. . . . In television we live and move and have our being."[19]

It is important for parents to remember that television has a tendency to destroy a family's interaction with each other. I have found that it is much easier to watch television than have a meaningful conversation with my kids. In this sense, even more than its subject matter, television destroys families because family members stop talking to each other and doing things with each other.

One of the things that I admire about my son Chris is his love for books. We read to all of our children when they were young, and while they all love to read today, Chris seemed to pick up on the joy of reading earlier than the others did. Today, I notice that Chris's conversations are alive and animated. He speaks with color in his descriptions. He writes regularly in his journal. He loves conversations about a broad range of subjects, and he is a delight to talk to. I think it is because he has spent more time practicing his communication skills and less time watching television. Because of this, he is a good connector with people, and he will be a good connector with his children someday.

Most parents know that "us three plus TV" is not connection. It is simply people who happen to be related, sitting in the same place, taking in images. I meet families who say they have regular mealtimes together, but they eat with the television on. Having dinner as a family while watching television is not really a meal together in the sense of sharing and communicating.

Years ago, life without modern media forced us to talk, relate, interact with each other. We had to read, tell stories, or sing songs to entertain each other. Today an entire world can be created without one stitch of togetherness. In his book *Leadership Is an Art,* Max Depree gives the account of his friend Dr. Carl Frost's experience while he was in Nigeria in the late sixties: "Electricity had just been brought into the village where he and his family were living. Each family got a single light in its hut. A real sign of progress. The trouble was that at night, though they had nothing to read and many of them did not know how to read, the families would sit in their huts in awe of this wonderful symbol of technology. The light-bulb watching began to replace the customary nighttime gatherings by the tribal fire, where the tribal storytellers, and elders, would pass along the history of the tribe. The tribe was losing its history in the light of a few electric bulbs."[20]

The same could be said for television in some homes. We teach our children what is valuable by the way we spend our time. Television is addictive. It can steal our time, hours of it. We need to reconsider how television is shaping our families' lives.

I. CHART WHAT YOU AND YOUR KIDS WATCH. For a two-week period of time, keep track of what each of you watches. Then evaluate whether or not this is the amount of time you want to be spending with the television. This can be a real eye-opener for your family.

2. PLAN WHAT YOU AND YOUR KIDS WATCH. Most parents plan meals and schedules, but most do not plan their family's television watching for the week. After you have discussed your television-watching charts and have discussed how much time you want to be watching television, set a specific plan of what and how much you will watch. Think of it as

planning a menu for the week: Choose nutritious programs with educational, spiritual, value-based content, and add a little dessert once in a while. Remember that what you feed your mind is what you are. One way to control what you watch is to watch videos that you know are wholesome.

3. EVALUATE WHAT YOU AND YOUR CHILDREN WATCH. When your children are watching television, sit and watch several programs with them to determine what programming is good for your kids. Talk to your children to see what they are perceiving and learning. Would you allow a stranger to come into your home and teach your children to hit and kick? Would you allow a stranger to come into your home and show your teenager sexually stimulating material? Well, that's exactly what we do if we let our children watch just anything on television.

4. IF YOU CAN'T CONTROL IT, KILL IT. If you find that you and your family cannot control your television watching, then consider getting rid of your television. If the television dominates your family's life, it will destroy your sense of connection.

🌿 Showing Compassion to Others

We cannot make the Kingdom of God happen,
    but we can put out leaves as it draws near.
We can be kind to each other. We can be kind to ourselves.
We can drive back the darkness a little.
We can make green places within ourselves and among
    ourselves
where God can make his Kingdom happen.
FREDERICK BUECHNER

ONE OF the most wonderful ways to connect with your children is by doing things together for others, expecting nothing in return. Modeling charity is a wonderful gift to bestow on your children.

My wife's father was a model of compassion. For many years he was faithful to visit the elderly in rest homes. Every week he drove 120 miles round-trip to Great Falls, Montana, to help people in the rescue mission. He always picked up hitchhikers. He frequently brought home a needy person for dinner. And he anonymously gave away hundreds of dollars each year to those who were going through hard times. He had a huge heart for people in need.

Something wonderful happens when we reach out to help others, to see the needs of others as more important than our own. It is a miracle: In giving, we receive. It is a divine principle, and it always works. The delight and joy that come from giving ourselves unselfishly to others are special feelings that cannot be duplicated any other way.

Our children need to know how to give to others, how to be compassionate, how to identify with the poor, the elderly, and the disadvantaged. They need to appreciate what struggles others may have to endure just to survive. Home is where we can learn the concept of compassion and charity—connecting with others in need.

All too often our children hear us make judgments of others. When we let go of our judgments and reach out to connect with others outside our immediate and comfortable circle, we take an important step toward being compassionate. Our children will both admire and model this virtue.

A few weeks ago, Nancie and Amy left the supermarket

after shopping for groceries, hurrying so they could get to church on time. Later, Nancie told me what happened. The early evening traffic was heavy as they waited to enter the highway. "Mom, look," Amy said softly, nodding toward a young woman who stood next to the car, holding a sign that said: "Hungry. Will work for food." Amy said, "Mom, can I give her the box of animal crackers I just bought?" They watched as the woman faced the heavy stream of traffic, an unreadable expression on her young face, maybe desperate bravado.

Nancie was about to explain to Amy that the woman's need was probably a ruse, that she most likely earned lots of money off people's guilt as they exited the grocery store. Instead, Nancie paused and then said, "I guess we could share some of our groceries."

They circled back in the parking lot and fixed up a bag of groceries, with Amy's box of animal crackers on top. They drove back to the woman, and as Amy handed her the bag, the woman began to cry. "God bless you," she said. Nancie and Amy left in tears too. What a simple thing—to give a hungry person food. But what a great lesson in compassion for Amy.

Charlotte Lunsford, national chairperson of volunteers for the Red Cross, says, "When people begin volunteering [for service] at a young age, normally they volunteer throughout their lives." We parents can cultivate the good ground of our homes by making them places that demonstrate Christ's compassion.

The New Testament reminds us of the deep bonding that goes on when we reach out to others. When we touch a needy person, we touch Jesus himself. "Come, you who are blessed by my Father, inherit the Kingdom prepared for you from the foundation of the world. For I was hungry, and you fed me. I was thirsty, and you gave me a drink. I was a stranger, and you invited me into your home. I was naked, and you gave me clothing. I was sick, and you cared for me. I was in prison, and you visited me."[21] The apostle James said, "Pure and lasting religion in the sight of God our Father means that we must care for orphans and widows in their troubles."[22]

HOME is the school for building relationships. Home teaches us how to get along with people and how to connect with others. There are no shortcuts. Words about connection won't work, and trying to substitute things instead of yourself in the connecting process will give your children the wrong message. Connection requires not only our time and effort but also our vulnerability. We must risk our own hearts to connect, but in the end, it is the only way we find family intimacy and connectedness.

And the rewards are great. Connected families express appreciation for each other. Connected families spend significant amounts of time together. Connected families possess better-than-average communication patterns. Connected families are committed to each other, even if it means personal sacrifice. Connected families practice compassion.[23]

TILLING THE GROUND
Questions for Thought and Reflection

As you think about how you can practice the habit of making your home a place of connection, record your thoughts in a journal or notebook. Then share your reflections with your spouse or a close friend, asking them to pray for you and help you to put into practice some of the things about which you have been convicted.

1. How does God bond to us? What can you do to strengthen the bond between you and your children?

2. How can you improve your communications skills with your spouse and children? Are you a good listener? Do you listen with your heart as well as your head? How would your children and spouse answer these two questions about you?

3. Do you make eye contact with your children when they speak to you? Do your children feel heard and understood?

4. Do you compliment your children verbally? Do you do this more often than you correct them verbally? Do you often tell them you love them?

5. How approachable are you? Do your children or your spouse often feel you are too busy or preoccupied? Do you spend more time doing your own thing than communicating and spending time with your family members?

6. Do your family members spend a significant amount of time relating to each other? (Remember, watching television together does not count.) What can you do to increase the quantity and quality of time you spend together?

7. Do you live close to members of your extended family (parents, grandparents, siblings, cousins, aunts, uncles)? Do you frequently visit with them? Do your children have a relationship with them? How can these family relationships help your children's sense of connection? Do you invest time and money in taking your children for a visit with geographically distant relatives such as grandparents?

8. List the things you do together as a family—daily, weekly, monthly, annually.

9. How often do you hug your children? What do you do to give healthy touch to your children?

10. If you are married, how does the quality of your marriage affect your children? In what ways do your children learn about commitment from you?

11. What can you do to bring more grace and forgiveness into your home?

12. How can you involve your children in acts and deeds of compassion?

CHAPTER 7

Legacy
Where Do I Belong?

Each of us contains
within our fragile vessels of skin and bones and cells
this inheritance of soul.
We are links between the ages,
containing past and present expectations,
sacred memories, and future promise.
Only when we recognize that we are heirs
can we truly be pioneers.

EDWARD C. SELLNER

🌿 Roots

I am the family face;
Flesh perishes, I live on,
Projecting trait and trace
Through time to times anon,
And leaping from place to place
Over oblivion.

THOMAS HARDY

IF THERE is a miracle in legacy, it is this: In the most profound way, I am connected to my great-grandparents to my grandparents to my parents to my children to my grandchildren, and on it goes. It is a unique history we pass on from generation to generation as part of our inheritance. Legacy speaks of who we are and what has gone before to pave the way. My legacy is my history.

Like an ancient fossil, my legacy leaves its unmistakable mark. I am billions of minute pieces of the tens of thousands of them—those who have gone before me. Because of them I belong to a group of someones who have been places, done things, thought thoughts, set up traditions, established mores, made families, and created a living culture as part of the race called human. They are mine, and I am theirs.

187

I am one of the now actors on the stage of this cast, this clan, bequeathing to mine what I have inherited from them: a name; the color of my eyes, hair, and skin; my abilities and interests; my physical capacities and personality traits; my culture; and my ideas. I am but a thread being woven into the fabric of this clan, and together we make a blanket that, no doubt, covers the world.

Legacy helps me know where I belong in the big scheme of things. It helps me know the pattern and fabric from which I am cut. I am attached not only to my immediate family members but also to a family tree with roots and history. The legacy I am weaving includes the others who have influenced me and my ancestors: prophets, teachers, mentors, friends, scoundrels, and heroes.

I am part of the act of the life of this clan, and the act continues on and on with millions of stories, some left untold forever. My tree includes my bloodline, my caregivers, my siblings, my friends, my mentors, my nation, my culture, my faith, and my race.

✒ My History

Voices call from unseen rooms
Echoing down the empty hall
Beckoning us to enter into
Worlds yet to be explored.
Sister, brother, parent, child,
Singing in the blood, singing in the bone,
Remember me, remember me.
MICHAEL E. WILLIAMS

MY STORY begins in the fields of Scotland. My name traces back to a parish in Chankerton, Lanarkshire, to an ancestor named Robert de Carmichael, who first appeared in 1220 when he resigned claim to the patronage of Cleghorn Church. He was known as "Lord of Cleghorn, a descendent of Walter Fitz Alan, who was appointed High Steward of Scotland by King David I, in 1130 A.D."

In 1789 Thomas Carmichael sailed for America with his wife, Mary, and their infant son. My great-great-grandfather, John H. Carmichael, was born that same year. Records show that Thomas had acquired land at Reedy Creek, Orange County, North Carolina. Eventually the family moved to Tennessee. John married Nancy Stalcup in 1819 when he was thirty and Miss Stalcup was eighteen. Over the next thirty years, she gave birth to twelve children, eight sons and four daughters. Their life was filled with prosperity and southern charm until war broke out between the North and the South.

It was a fateful time in America's history to be having sons of eligible age to fight in wars. By February 1, 1861, North Carolina, Virginia, South Carolina, Mississippi, Florida, Alabama, Georgia, Louisiana, and Texas had passed ordinances of secession. By May, Arkansas and Tennessee had joined the Confederate effort, and the Civil War was raging. I can only imagine Nancy's concern since several of her sons were fighting for the South.

Before a year had passed, she had already lost two sons. Nashville had been taken over by the Union army. One of Nancy's neighbors (known as "Miss A.M.B." from her diaries) wrote,

Saturday, the 15th of February, was a rainy, drizzling,
sleeting, chilly day, when the bell tolled from our market
house, ordering the citizens to assemble in solemn
conclave. . . . The Confederate forces were retreating South,
and no citizen was allowed to cross the bridge until the army
were over. Hurried words of parting were said by the young
men who stopped at their homes, while many mothers
pressed the manly forms of their sons to their hearts for the
last time and printed a good-bye kiss on their lips, while the
tears choked their utterance.[1]

My great-great-grandmother was no doubt among those
tearful mothers. Two of her sons, Hance and William, were
among the Confederate soldiers retreating. As the war
dragged on, conditions worsened. Rebeccah Ridley wrote in
her diary from Jefferson, Tennessee, in December 1863,

We have had severe sleet for three days. The ground has
been covered with snow and ice—freezing our poor
unprotected soldiers—some of them I understand are
barefooted, none have tents—or a sufficiency of blankets
and all have to depend on the country for subsistence—poor
fellows, how my heart bleeds for them.[2]

Before the war ended, both Hance and William became two
more of the six hundred thousand Civil War casualties. Four of
John and Nancy's eight sons were killed in the ravages of one
bloody war, perishing in the losing cause to preserve slavery and
free the South from the North. It was a dark time in the history
of America and a dark time in the Carmichael family.

John and Nancy's tenth child, Jesse, my great-grand-
father, was one of the four remaining sons who had been
spared during the war. In 1868, after the war had ended,
Jesse helped his family gather up what was left of their lives
and moved with them to California. By then Jesse, age twenty-
six, was married to a twenty-two-year-old beauty named
Winnie, the daughter of Rev. Henry B. Johnson.

At the time of their move by train to Sonoma County
near San Francisco, Jesse and Winnie had a one-year-old son
named William Lafayette Carmichael. He would later become
my grandfather. In 1900 he married his third cousin, Nancy
Elizabeth Johnson.

William and Nancy had a pretty good life, both living into
their eighties. They had six children. Harold, their fifth child
and second oldest son, was born in 1911. Harold became very
ill with typhoid fever when he was three and with a burst
appendix when he was seven. On both occasions he was very
near death, but my Grandma Carmichael would later tell me
that she knew God had spared Harold for a very special reason—and that just maybe, part of that special reason was me.
Harold was my father.

My grandfather owned a vineyard in Dinuba, California,
and my father speaks fondly of his childhood, of the wonderful
farmhouse, of sleeping on the screened porch during warm
summer nights, of hunting and fishing trips up into the Sierra
mountains, and of watching his mother churn butter and bake
fruit pies. But when the Great Depression hit the farmers in
1926, it was all they could do to hang on. By 1927 they had
lost the farm.

My mother came from a blended family. My Grandmother

Thomas had two children from a previous marriage when she met my grandfather. My grandfather was an alcoholic, and yet my mother has fond memories of him. So do I. When my mother was a child, none of her family had any spiritual awareness. But a godly next-door neighbor named Mrs. Cook often invited the Thomas children over for warm cookies and milk. She also took them to church. It was through her influence that my Uncle Floyd and eventually all of the other children, including my mother, Betty, became Christians. Two of her brothers later became missionaries.

When my Grandpa Carmichael lost the farm, the family moved to San Jose, where twenty-six-year-old Harold met sixteen-year-old Betty Thomas and fell in love. My father was accused of "robbing the cradle" by others in the church where they met, but he did not care what they said. Nearly sixty years later, he still looks at her with that sparkle and undying love he felt for her when they were married in February 1938.

At 4:55 A.M. on January 13, 1943, I, William Leland, a fourth-generation William, was born into this clan, this tribe, this branch of history, this legacy. My family includes farmers, inventors, missionaries, soldiers, carpenters, preachers, lawyers, doctors, college professors, fighter pilots, blue-collar workers, and thousands of devoted mothers and fathers. It also includes murderers, eccentrics, drunks, and thieves.

In my natural past there are both heroes and villains. I am related to a great missionary—my mother's brother Floyd Thomas, who brought hope and healing to Africa. I also know that I am related through my mother to Samuel Morse, who invented the Morse code. But then my father tells me about a great-uncle who was stabbed with a pitchfork by an angry man who caught my great-uncle in bed with the man's wife. My history gives me the perspective that what I do now will affect not just my children but also generations of children. The things I teach and model, just like the genes I pass on, will carry meaning and habit to future generations. It means my actions and work in building character will have an impact on my children and on thousands of people in the generations of my descendants. The blood that flows in my veins goes back for centuries, and it will be carried forward for generations to come. When I think about who I am in this way, I am awestruck. I am the present, living, breathing expression of this "cloud of witnesses" who have gone on before, and I can visualize those who will come after me to carry on the pulse and lifeblood of this family.

What have I learned? What is the collective voice of experience saying to me? What truth does my history speak to my children? What are the lessons of life being whispered to me through the legacy of my ancestors? Sometimes in my visualization of this, I think that if I turn my head in either direction and glance quickly enough, I will see them there. They and their claim to life and this family are so real.

What is your family history? How has that history shaped you? What stories in your past give meaning, teach lessons, or inspire hope? Some people do not know it. Some do not want to know their past, or at least they claim not to want to know it. But I believe that inside all of us is a yearning to know more about who we are.

Our daughter, Amy, adopted from Korea, wants to know.

Adopted children have an extra legacy. Some think of adoptees as having less legacy. But in reality, they have more. They have a bloodline by birth and a family by adoption. Amy is curious about both. She has been quizzing her mother lately about her Grandpa Pearson. Nancie's father died before Amy became a part of our family. Clearly she views him as part of her ancestry now that she has been thoroughly bonded into our family. She also has interest in her Korean heritage, and we plan to take her there someday and help her discover as much as we can about that part of her kinship.

Some people want to bury the dark side of their past and therefore never speak of their legacy. Some are ashamed of it. Others are angry with it. Still others have been wounded by it. But I believe all of our history is important. We can learn from it all. While the psalmist David was a great man of faith and leadership, he was also an adulterer and murderer. The stories of his sins are told in graphic detail. By today's laws, he would have been imprisoned for life or put to death for the murder of Bathsheba's first husband. By Old Testament Levitical law, he would have been put to death for his adulterous behavior. Neither happened. God's grace intervened. And that is what makes the dark side a good memory. If we learn from dark ancestral pasts that behaviors have consequences and that there is hope from God's grace, we have learned a great deal.

As parents, we are a vital part of the legacy we leave for our children and our children's children for many generations. What will that legacy look like based on how we are living today and the choices that we make? What will our family history say of us in the years to come?

✒ Embracing Our Past

There are places we all come from—
deep-rooty-common places—that make us who we are.
And we disdain them or treat them lightly at our peril.
We turn our backs on them at the risk of self-contempt.
There is a sense in which we need to go home again—
and can go home again.
Not to recover home, no. But to sanctify memory.

ROBERT FULGHUM

MY FIRST college experience was at a small, private
Christian college located in the mountains of Santa Cruz,
California. Bethany College is surrounded by beautiful red-
woods and seemed to my parents an ideal place to stick an
immature seventeen-year-old who had not taken academics
very seriously up to that point. My mother had begged me
to go there, saying, "Please, just give it a year, if for nothing
else than to get grounded in the Bible." And so I went, not
so much because of her begging, but because I really had no
other goals in life. It was a big step for a kid who had tried to
get his mother to let him quit school after finishing the
eighth grade.

At the time, this unaccredited college would admit virtually
anyone who could qualify for a student loan and sign the statement of faith. I could do both, so it was not hard for me to get
admitted, even though I had pretty bad grades from high school.

I was there only a few weeks before I realized that even in
this strict, private religious college, I had more freedom than
I had ever experienced before. Mom Swanson, the elderly
dean of women, kept a watch on campus romances like an
ardent Doberman. We had to have date slips to take a girl out.

To do this, we would go into Mom Swanson's office the afternoon of the intended date, sit across from her at her desk, and
answer interrogating questions as she peered over her bifo-
cals and filled in the date slip, keeping a carbon copy for her
records.

"Now, where are you going?" she would quiz.

"Oh, just to get something to eat," was my reply the first
time I applied.

"Well, that should not take more that forty-five minutes,
so I will give you permission to be gone together for one hour.
What time are you leaving?" If you were not back at the
appointed time, you were in big trouble. The idea, of course,
was to keep young people in the peak of hormonal passion
from falling into sin while idly parked at the beach. From what
I observed, this system didn't work very well.

I soon learned to go into Mom Swanson's office with a
whole list of activities planned: "We are going to dinner, then
to a Bible study, and then on to play miniature golf, and then,
I don't know, maybe stop at the drive-in for a Coke before we
come home." I could never imagine saying to her, "And then
we want to park in some secluded romantic place!" She was
suspicious, and for good reason, but it always worked in getting a date slip for about three hours.

That first year I made many friends. I was enjoying every
minute of my social life. I was my own boss. Like most seventeen-
year-olds, I wanted to be my own man, free from people telling
me what to do.

When I was a sophomore, my parents moved to Santa
Cruz and ruined my life. They built a new house within three
blocks of the college. I don't know if they wanted to be closer

to me or if they wanted to live in the area or if they merely wanted to make my life miserable. All I know is it spoiled all my fun. My parents started to pressure me to move home to save money. Even worse, my mother got a job on campus working at The Spot, which was the student commons and popular social hangout.

Young men of eighteen like to think that they are independent, that they have successfully jettisoned all of their familial past, and that they are genuine originals. To have my mother hanging around The Spot, fixing my buddies hamburgers and fries and socializing with all of the girls on campus, really put a crimp in my new lifestyle.

On occasion, when I came home, my mother wanted to talk about the kids on campus and what I thought of particular people. Mom acted as if she were one of us! All I wanted was to rid myself of my past. I wanted my parents out of the picture. I did not want my friends associating me with any of my family, especially the one who gave birth to me, the one from whose breasts I received nourishment as an infant! This was awful.

My mother knew more about me–the people I spent time with and where I spent my time–than I ever wanted her to know. "What did you do Saturday night?" she'd ask. The typical teenage answer of "Oh, nothing" didn't work because she had names and facts to quiz me about. And if I was too evasive, she would increase her detective work while on duty at The Spot by quizzing my friends about me. It forced me to reveal things college boys traditionally don't tell their mothers. It made me a miserable guy to live with.

Hence, during my sophomore year, I began to avoid both

my mother and The Spot. Obviously this hurt my mother deeply. She did not understand why I was treating her as if she had leprosy. I was struggling for independence, and she was grasping to continue being included in my life. The two objectives were totally incompatible.

Having my parents come back into my life made me cruel and cranky. Nothing suited me then. My parents looked old-fashioned and out-of-date. I saw myself stuck in a family I did not like. I wanted to be something different, something more, but mainly I wanted to do things without having my parents know.

I have now discovered that as much as we try to escape our roots, being our own person means eventually embracing those roots. It is only through our particular roots that we enter into life, and it is only through our particular roots that we pass life on. If we are to understand anything about ourselves and our station in life, we will need to come to peace with our legacy. Writer and storyteller Garrison Keillor said, "Some luck lies in not getting what you thought you wanted but getting what you have, which once you have it you may be smart enough to see is what you would have wanted had you known."[3] Keillor is right. We are who we are because of our roots, our family. When we finally embrace and come to terms with our legacy, we can begin on the road to building a life for ourselves.

But eighteen-year-olds have not discovered this yet. We can't discover it yet because we are still letting go and being let go. We must free ourselves before we can come back to embrace what we tried to get rid of. And so we struggle to shed our heritage like a snake shedding its skin. Some shedding attempts are more violent than others. It is not only painful for the child who is flailing about to be free; it is also painful for the parent.

I have watched our older children go through the same process. M. Scott Peck speaks truth to every parent's heart in his book *In Search of Stones* when he says, "However well we may have trained ourselves to care for [our children], and however many years we may have exercised that care, there comes a time, gradually or suddenly, subtly or dramatically, when we need to step aside. It's impossible to know how to do it right. Children are likely to blame us for doing it too soon or too late, too gently or too abruptly. They are unlikely to have any appreciation for how difficult it may be for their parents to drastically change roles. But so what? It's not an issue of ease. It's simply of what needs to be done."[4] As parents it is our job to let go. But as children, it is our privilege to return and embrace our roots.

I now have a better appreciation for my roots. Much of the inspiration for this book comes from my roots. I consider my family history a rich wellspring. Family history is like a landmark, giving us a larger sense of time and place. As Elizabeth Berg says in *Family Traditions,* "It can give us a feeling like we get when we lie on our backs looking at the stars."[5]

🌿 Coming to Grips with Our Own Mortality
Our children are living messages we send to a time and place we will never see.
UNKNOWN

I REMEMBER the first time the idea of mortality hit me. The year was 1950. I was seven years old, and my father was building a house for a family in our town. Just days before, I had helped my father clean up wood scraps at the new Detliff house on a Saturday afternoon. Mr. Detliff had been there with his son Gary, who attended school with me. John Detliff was a kind man and always took time to speak with me. I liked that, and I liked him. On a flight to Denver to attend his mother's funeral, Mr. Detliff's plane crashed in the Colorado mountains. My father, not knowing this, had gone to the house to fix a door. He rang the doorbell and asked if he could come in to fix the door. Mrs. Detliff said, "Oh, not today, Harold. We have just received news that John's plane crashed. We think he died. . . ." Her voice trailed off in tears as my father told her how sorry he was.

When I heard about this from my father, I was shocked. "The plane went down in a snowstorm over the rugged mountains near the Wyoming border. It hit so hard it bounced over into Colorado," he said. My seven-year-old mind was wrestling with this reality for the first time. Just two days earlier I had spoken with Mr. Detliff, laughed with him, and now he was dead. How did Gary feel? What would dying on an airplane feel like? Did he die right away? Did he scream just before impact like people in the movies did? It all seemed so stark and final. John Detliff dead.

Our culture has made death a distant and morbid thing rather than a natural thing. A PBS special portrayed how a tribe in South America handled the death of one young woman. She lay in a hammock while her mother and sisters braided her hair and decorated the body with paints and flowers. The tribal chief admonished the relatives to cry and mourn more loudly. Finally some of the tribal men built a box-like log fire. At the appointed moment, the woman's body, still in the hammock, was laid into the fire, and more wood was stacked on top. The entire tribe squatted around the fire and wailed as the fire burned everything to ashes. These people touched and fondled their dead and watched them go up in smoke.

We in our culture think of that as primitive. Most people die in hospitals, and undertakers take away the corpses. Our "remains" are not ever again in the care of our loved ones. We teach our children nothing about death in school. The only dead people we witness are on television or in the movies.

Rather than treating death as a normal part of life, we treat it as an unexpected crisis, a thing that happens when modern medicine fails. People always die of something—some disease or body failure—never just in their due time.[6] To us, death is unnatural. We have billion-dollar industries that help us trick ourselves about the aging process and lie to us about getting younger rather than older. As a result, deaths are "unexpected," and families are basically at a loss about what to do.

Jesus spoke often of death, not only his own, but also of the certainty that life here was but a temporary prelude to eternity. He and his disciples clearly saw something joyful and hopeful about death.

Death is part of life. To refuse to speak of it, to fail to put it into perspective for our children, to fail to plan for it is a mistake. Our own mortality is an important component of knowing who we are. It gives us a perspective that is necessary if we are to age with grace and understanding, if we are to embrace all of the stages of life, if we are to treasure our days, if we are to prepare for eternity. Have you ever noticed that when people find out they have a limited time to live, they start living better? They begin to reorganize their life in new ways. That's what happens when we begin to embrace death as part of life.

When Nancie's father died of cancer, our two oldest sons, then ages ten and eight, attended the funeral. They viewed their grandpa's body, cold and lifeless in the casket. They asked me many questions. "Was that really him? Could he hear us now? Why did he feel cold to the touch? Was he in heaven? Where is heaven? What made him die? What happens to us when we die? Will I die?" In a simple way, we had some wonderful conversations about our mortality, about generations, about our time on earth, about love and memories that can never die, about making our lives count for something, and about where we would like to spend eternity.

Nancie loves to visit old cemeteries. I have kind of picked up the habit with her. We have stopped along the road more than once to read the inscriptions on the tombstones of the dead in a pioneer cemetery. "Mary Ann Miller, born December 4, 1881, died June 12, 1882. We will always love you darling," on one tombstone. What was the story behind this infant's death? How did the parents feel? How did they cope? "Henry McFadden, 1856–1955." Wow! Ninety-nine years. What did he do with all that time? Did he have children? How many wives did he outlive? And then there are the ones that tell you something more. "Jessica Singleton, 1895–1922. Died giving birth to Raymond." I wonder how Raymond lived his life knowing this?

Epicurus said, "The art of living well and dying well are one." Cemeteries are repositories of the epic of humanity. I think it helps our perspective to visit there once in a while.

Cemeteries can provoke ponderous thoughts about life, and so can other things—waiting for the biopsy results to come back, mourning with your child whose teenage friend was killed in a drunk-driving accident, going through a divorce or a bankruptcy. These bring the daily drone of life to a screeching halt while we think about what gives meaning to life. Don't dismiss these thoughts as morbid quite so quickly. They are an important part of knowing who you are and where you want to go.

When we face our own mortality, we gain a new appreciation for the priceless gift of life. In realizing the absolute certainty of death, we tend to take life less seriously, enjoying even the frivolous moments. We in turn tend to take God much more seriously. The prospect of death seems to help us take time to smell the roses and treat others with more forgiveness and tolerance. In those reflective moments, the immense magnitude of life, going on before me and proceeding after me, seems bigger than the Montana sky. In the context of death, memories become more precious, and the important lessons we were taught from those we love seem to come back with an exclamation mark.

Telling Stories

The real histories of families aren't the records
of births, deaths, and marriages.
They are the stories told after dessert,
when the coffee's been served and everyone's too full to move.
FREDERICK WATERMAN

CHILDREN love stories because storytelling is a God-shaped expression of the soul. God chose to communicate himself through a story—the story of the nation of Israel and the story of his Son. Jesus taught his disciples essential truths with stories. Elie Wiesel said, "God made man because he loves stories."[7] Image and imagination are powerful forces in our lives from the time we can begin to think and communicate.

One of the best gifts I have ever received was given to me by my mother. She gave me my Aunt Hazel's diaries. Aunt Hazel was one of my father's sisters. She was eighty-four when she died from Alzheimer's disease seven years ago. After she died, my Uncle Raymond gave my mother fifteen years of his wife's diaries dating from 1933 to 1948. Two years ago, my mother gave them to me.

Frankly, in reading these diaries, I can't quite figure out why she kept them. Most of the daily entries are notations about what time she got up, where she went, what she had for dinner, and what time she went to bed. But I decided to read through them anyway since I felt I would learn something of my history in reading them. I'm glad I did because I found some great treasures.

JANUARY 13, 1943

> Billy [that's me] was born at 4:55 A.M. this morning at O'Connor's [hospital]. Harold and Betty [that's my mom and dad] brought Charlene [that's my sister] over at quarter to one this morning and Betty's baby was born four hours later.

JANUARY 21, 1943

> Harold took Betty and Billy home from hospital. I went by after work to see Billy. He sure is darling.

FEBRUARY 7, 1943

> Harold and Betty had Billy dedicated at church this morning.

There you have it, documentation of my birth, my good looks, and my dedication to almighty God! I found other tidbits in there, like my Aunt Hazel's aggravation at my father's driving habits:

> Harold drove my new car to San Francisco and went ninety miles per hour the whole way.

She never gave much personal opinion and rarely told us how she was feeling about things. She never spoke philosophically.

Big news stories were taken in stride with her daily routine. On December 7, 1941, her word-for-word entry was,

> Japan bombed Pearl Harbor today, sunk the U.S. Lexington and killed about 3,000 people in the Hawaiian Islands. She declared war on us. Sis Pierce, Jack Kerr and mother Kerr come over in afternoon. Cecil and Florence went to church with us in morning.

There were a few more entries about "war excitement" and "blackouts" a few days later, but that was all regarding World War II.

As I read through days of mundane entries, I learned something else about my family. They loved big dinner parties. In one January entry Aunt Hazel wrote,

> We had lunch at Eva's. She had heart and tongue and custard pie with whipped cream. LaVern came over after work and stayed for supper. Had waffles, sausage, and eggs. Then had freezer ice cream and cake.

The very next day her entry was,

> Was sick all morning with stomach flu. Mother was sick too. We all vomited and went to bed.

On Valentine's Day of 1943 she wrote,

> Everybody had Sunday dinner at our place. Cooked ten pounds of roast beef. Viola and Betty brought three pies each and a salad. Took Ray to the hospital in evening about 5:30.

Aunt Hazel never put it together. These poor people were making themselves sick with mountains of fatty foods at their feasts! No wonder there is a weight problem in my family. When I read this to my kids, we laughed until we cried.

Writer Michael E. Williams describes how stories are powerful in transmitting our legacy. "Storytelling is a form of the ancient communal spiritual discipline of hospitality. It is a continual process of transforming sojourners into kinfolk and strangers into friends. The voice of the story resonates from deep within the body and imagination of its teller, and its vibrations reach into the physical and imaginative depths of the listener. The images that linger on the outskirts of consciousness and the voices that continue to sound in the ear of the heart are the threads that connect us to those who have known and loved the story across the ages. To be invited into the world of a story is to be offered the hospitality of the community of people who live by that story." He goes on to say, "Anyone who tells a story speaks a world into being."[8]

When we tell our stories, we are not only communicating our legacy but also helping ourselves shape our life's message. By telling our stories, we recount and relive and reflect. It is a necessary way to help us find ourselves. Sue Monk Kidd says, "Without such stories we cannot be fully human, for without them we are unable to articulate or even understand our deepest experiences."[9] The meaning of life comes alive as we put it into story form.

When we tell stories, we create images in the minds of our listeners and take them places they have never been before. We invite them to share in our visions and landscapes. By telling our stories, we tell our listeners that we trust them to belong to us. As they enter our worlds, they become like kinfolk. A small piece of us is deposited in their memory and imagination. By exchanging our stories, we carry parts of ourselves into the other's legacy.

You do not need to write a book or create a Broadway play to tell your story. It can be done piece by piece as you live out your life. Journaling will help, and having regular storytelling rituals within your family and intimate circle will help. Turning off the television will help. Reading books to your children about other people's stories will help. Letting stories happen to you and looking for them in your everyday life will help. Talking to your parents and searching your history will help. Recordings and picture albums will help. But in the end, it will be you who tells the story.

Stories are the most effective way to transmit your faith to your children. When you tell your personal stories of faith and God's working in your life, you bring the Bible and your faith from a legend to a living reality. Tell the story of how you found God, how he works in your life and the lives of other Christians around you. Put the Bible stories into your own words. Tell about David and Goliath with great pomp and color. Let the stories live! Your stories will form the foundation for your children's belief in God.

Remember, too, that stories will transmit a conscience for morality. When moral truth is communicated through stories, our children see it as more than keeping rules. Stories illustrate the dynamic truth and value of the virtues we want them to live. Even the truth of the Word of God is set in the stories found throughout its pages. Your children need stories in order to catch the vision of the way things ought to be.[10]

Storytelling is the most powerful way to transmit your legacy to your children. It will certainly help them feel they belong. Inside each of us lies a storyteller and a unique story. Discover your story, and share it with your children.

🌿 Belonging to Each Other

My prayer is not for the world,
but for those you have given me,

because they belong to you.
And all of them, since they are mine, belong to you;
and you have given them back to me,
so they are my glory!
JESUS' PRAYER FOR HIS DISCIPLES, JOHN 17:9-10

WE ALL desperately want to belong. It is a basic human
need. Going shopping with your children for school clothes
will give you a great illustration of how badly kids want to
belong. Our children all played basketball. From the time they
were in the fourth grade, they knew the difference between
basketball shoes and *the* basketball shoes. Skor or Puma were
inferior brands. No, they wanted Nikes, and not just the
$49.95 Nikes. They just *had to have* the $99.95 Air Jordan
Nikes. And Levi 501s were the jeans to wear. Heaven forbid
that Mom would bring home some Wrangler jeans. "Wrangler
is what the cowboy crowd wears, Mom. And I am *not* in that
group!" they would plead.

Our daughter, Amy, and her mom still go one or two
rounds on many school mornings about Amy's desire for the
"baggy" look. Amy loves wearing oversized clothes since it is
the "in" thing to do. Nancie hates it and thinks it speaks of
some kind of rebellious crowd. And so the battle goes on.
Most of this tug-of-war about clothing falls into the category
of a child's need to belong. I suspect that if we adults stopped
to think about it, a lot of what we do is also driven by the need
to belong.

We are a species of belongers. We all belong to a variety
of denominations, social clubs, organizations, neighborhoods, and small groups that make us feel comfortable and
feed our need to belong. We bunch up, we group, we invent

all kinds of ways and reasons to be together, to belong. Human beings were not created to be isolated from each other. It is instinctive.

The family is the basic group of belonging. It is the most intimate of groups to which we belong. It is the group that knows the most about us and loves us anyway. Our society has strong feelings about the bond of belonging. Traditionally, our legal system will not tear children away from their parents if it is at all possible to keep them together. Mothers usually have priority because of the basic sense of belonging to the one who birthed you. When a child gets lost in a shopping mall, the security guard will ask, "Who do you belong to?" When the parent claims the child, the parent often says, "He belongs to me." When that sense of belonging to one's family breaks down, children find gangs and other strong alliances that transcend the bond of family. Sadly, a lot of today's children do not feel that they belong to their families.

There are many ways we can transmit to our children a sense that they belong. Lewis Smedes in the book *Shame and Grace* wrote, "The difference between owning and possessing comes down to this; we possess things, but we own persons. . . . Possession is control; ownership is commitment." Smedes goes on to say that we show ownership (what I would call a sense of belonging) in three ways. "Taking responsibility: I respond to my child's deep need to be owned with a commitment that we will always belong to each other; Feeling pride: I am eager to let the world know that this child and I belong to each other; Finding joy: I am grateful and elated that this wondrous human being is here with me and I am here with her."[11]

Shared history is another way we give children a sense of
belonging. If children feel connected to their family, if they
feel they have roots, they will feel a greater sense of belonging.
This is done by sharing our history, by telling the legends of
the family, and by performing rituals together. We draw enor-
mous strength from the sense of belonging.

Legacy gives us that sense of stability, of continuity, of
permanence. Our shared story bonds and unites us. It helps
us hold together in a world swirling with change and uncer-
tainty. I belong, therefore I have a core, a center to which I
can anchor myself. Belonging creates a deep sense of personal
worth and value because I am kept, treasured, and cherished.

None of us really knows exactly how this sense of belonging happens, but we all know the good and secure feeling we
get when it does. We feel part of the "in" group. To have an
innate sense for one another, to perceive when one of our
members is ill or feeling down, to discern when something is
going wrong, to let them in on the secrets and code words of
the group, to feel known and still loved, to have a shared
vision—these all convey a sense of belonging to the members
of our family.

What we mean to each other as family is not an abstract. It
is specific lives, born in a particular order. Families represent
a physical and spiritual togetherness that plays its unmistakable part in who we are and who we become. Our family is like
a cast of characters. We all play our parts in the soap operas,
comedies, tragedies, and epics of our lives. We do not choose
our part, and we cannot assume another's part. We are who
we are, and our family becomes either a launching pad or a
millstone. We can never fully become the unique individuals

God intends until we can root that individuality in the legacy bequeathed to us.

In his book *A Pretty Good Person,* Lewis Smedes said, "The strongest and brightest of us are fragile as a floating bubble, unsteady as a newborn kitten on a waxed kitchen floor. If we keep our footing in the shaky space between our arrival and departure from this world, we owe our survival—not to mention our success—to many other people who held us up and helped us crawl or fly or just muck our way through." [12]

🌿 Giving Children a Lasting Inheritance

I know that you sincerely trust the Lord,
for you have the faith of your mother, Eunice,
and your grandmother, Lois.
THE APOSTLE PAUL WRITING TO TIMOTHY, 2 TIMOTHY 1:5

NANCIE and I have been married for thirty years. We have lived together much longer than we lived apart before being married. Obviously we know each other pretty well. It is amazing to observe in Nancie things that I can directly attribute to her parents. Certain expressions remind me of her father; other habits remind me of her mother. Her love for the earth was bequeathed to her from her farmer father. For her, smelling the freshly plowed earth is like smelling a bit of heaven. Her love for books was bequeathed to her from her mother, a writer and reader who treasured the ideas and stories of good authors and who took regular trips to the library with her children.

I sometimes see Nancie's dad when she smiles and hear

her mom when she speaks. She is not only a composite of mother and father and all of the ancestral bloodline that went into her parents; she is also made up of other people: Elmer Schwoch, a marvelous mentor-teacher from her tiny one-room country schoolhouse; Uncle Kenny and Aunt Julia, who visited the farm each summer, spreading their wit and humor; and a thousand others who inhabited the little farming town of Conrad, Montana. All of them served up a small piece of the person who is my wonderful wife. She is their legacy and an inheritor of their lives.

When we hear the word *inheritance,* we often think of money. We hear stories of people who are left a small fortune by a forgotten great-uncle or tales of the widow who left her fortune to her housekeeper. But inheritance is much deeper than material wealth. It is who we are, both good and bad. Our physical characteristics, our personality traits, and much of our fundamental belief system are inherited from our parents and significant others who touched our lives while we were young.

Think about it. Every day we add something to the list of things we pass down to our children. Each of our children will receive either by design or default a fundamental belief system of the way things ought to be and the habits that control our lives. It is a mistake for parents to think that there is any neutral zone here. Every day we teach either constructive characteristics and habits or potentially destructive ones. For most of us, it is a combination of both. Inheritance is not a one-time monumental thing. It is not like reading the deceased father's will and discovering he left his children millions of dollars.

Inheritance happens slowly, little piece by little piece, routine day by routine day. The food we fix and serve teaches something about nutrition or lack of it. The vocabulary we use teaches something about grace or vulgarity. The tone of voice and the things we choose to say teach something about compassion or abuse. The places we go, the movies we watch, the friends we associate with, the things we care enough to argue about, the groups and associations we join, the volunteer work we do or don't do, the churches we attend, the prayers we say or don't say, the attitudes we display toward education and the environment, the way we treat our spouses, our neighbors, our pets, our children—a thousand things and more add up to a way of life we are passing on to our children. Whatever it is, it is the biggest part of their inheritance.

I confess I would like to leave my children something in the way of a financial inheritance. I would enjoy knowing that somehow they are providing for their families, and I would gain satisfaction from having some part in helping them accomplish this. However, when I was a young parent, I did not consciously consider the fact that I was, at that moment, passing on something far more significant. I was weaving into them a view of life and a set of emotional tools to assist them in coping with whatever life would bring their way. I was helping to build the walls of character, stone by stone. What they received then has influenced how well they are navigating life today.

At best, I handed down a variety of mixed blessings to my children. When I die, my children will probably sift through all the letters, photos, books, and journals I leave. Already they are sifting through the ideas, principles, and ideals I taught them, picking the ones that mean something to them, interpreting them for their own lives, and throwing the rest away. That is the human nature at work. But a lot of what they keep will depend on what Nancie and I have left them. I have been thinking about this lately as I watch my grown children establishing their lives.

When I think about what I want my children and grandchildren to inherit from me, financial assets are last on the list. First, I want my children to inherit a faith in the God of Abraham, Isaac, and Jacob. I want them to inherit a God who answers prayer and gives grace to sinners. I want them to realize that while God has no grandchildren, they can discover God as their heavenly Father through a personal relationship with Jesus Christ.

Next, I would like my children to inherit their grandparents' and parents' commitment to their marriage and family. I want them to place their family above their work, their play, their success, and their personal gratification. I want them to be examples of love and integrity.

I want them to inherit their Grandpa Pearson's work ethic and simple vision of the way things ought to be. I want them to take pleasure and delight in the little things, to love the land, to reach out to widows and orphans, and to love the church and God's people.

I would also like my children to inherit their Uncle Bob's achievement dream that includes much more than money, fame, or power— a dream that includes a life committed to character and principle.

I want them to inherit their mother's compassion and joy

in giving to others. I want them to be at every turn and every chance hilarious givers. I want them to inherit their father's ability to take risks, dream dreams, and follow those dreams.

I want them to inherit their Grandpa Carmichael's contagious sense of humor and optimism, to realize that life is a great adventure and that those you love are to be cherished and enjoyed. I want them to take the time to pray as he prays.

I want them to inherit their Great-Uncle Floyd's ability to do the noble thing, like being a missionary or a teacher, some kind of loyal service that makes the world a better place and builds the kingdom of God.

I want them to inherit their Grandma Pearson's sense of wonder and creativity, seeing goodness and beauty all around. I want them to inherit their Grandma Carmichael's constant caring and staying in touch—qualities that hold families together. I want them to inherit her sense of hospitality, giving joy through simple things like warm bread and freshly baked cookies.

From all of us, I want them to inherit a moral compass that gives them clear direction and distinction between right and wrong, good and evil. Finally, I want them to inherit a collective sense of hope, a belief that life is essentially good and that even in suffering and hardship we can feel sunshine and a sense of purpose.

My friend, editor and writer David Kopp, shared this touching personal story of inheritance. "On a rainy Saturday afternoon, friends and relatives gathered in a small chapel to watch as my children, smiling and excited, stepped into the waters. We listened as Uncle Tom led each in their confession of faith: 'Neil, tell us when Jesus Christ became your

Lord.' 'Taylor, what does baptism mean?' 'Jana, how will you keep on growing in Christ?' We applauded as each child came up—wet, pink and shining, like newborns. Then we sang 'Great Is Thy Faithfulness,' and Grandma Kopp closed with a prayer to the One who had opened their hearts. At that moment, it seemed to me our family was passing on the real inheritance."[13] Yes, they were!

HOME is a circle. It moves from generation to generation, each one linking us to a legacy like a chain. It is an endless lineage of birthing, nurturing, teaching, growing, chronicling, changing, aging, and dying. Home is handing down the bloodline, the gene pool, the heritage, the memories, the stories, the history, and the traditions. It is a family. It is *my* family.

TILLING THE GROUND
Questions for Thought and Reflection

As you think about how you can practice the habit of making your home a place of legacy, record your thoughts in a journal or notebook. Then share your reflections with your spouse or a close friend, asking them to pray for you and help you to put into practice some of the things about which you have been convicted.

1. What do you know about your family history, your family tree, your ancestry?
2. What stories do you remember being told about your family when you were a child? What do you recall about your parents, grandparents, aunts, uncles, siblings, teachers, friends, places you lived, etc.?
3. What events in your life make up your personal history? What have those things taught you about life and living?

4. Do you feel good about your past and your family history? What things in your past have you avoided telling or have you edited out of your past? Why? Will you tell your children these things someday? Why or why not?

5. Have you shared with your children stories about how God is working in your life or has helped you in the past? Have you talked about how you came to believe in God? Have you told your children the story of how you found your spouse?

6. Have you told your children about their birth—how you felt when they were born, who was there to witness their birth, etc.?

7. Have you thought much about death? Are they healthy thoughts? Are you comfortable with the idea that death will happen someday, or do you fear death? What are you conveying to your children about death and dying? Has any close family member died? How did you cope with that, and how did you express it to your children?

8. Do your family members tell stories? What can you do to improve your storytelling skills? Do you regularly read stories to your children? Do you have a good collection of stories that teach valuable lessons about life? How often do you read the Bible together? Do you have a contemporary "living" translation or a children's version of the Bible that is easy for your children to understand?

9. Do you keep a personal journal? If not, have you considered starting one?

10. What kind of inheritance do you hope to leave your children? Write down a list of what you would like to leave to your children.

CHAPTER 8

Purpose
Why Am I Here?

Where am I? Who am I?
How did I come to be here?
What is this thing called the world?
How did I come into the world?
Why was I not consulted?
And if I am compelled to take part in it,
Where is the director?
I want to see him.

SØREN KIERKEGAARD

✒ Why *am* I Here?

What our deepest self craves is not more enjoyment
but some supreme purpose
that will give unity and direction to our life.
We can never know the profoundest joy
without a conviction that our life is significant—
not a meaningless episode.
KENNY J. GOLDRING

WHEN I was a kid, I would sometimes think about eternity. I tried to think about a God with no beginning and no end. "If he had no beginning, where did he come from, and how did he get there?" I asked my mom.

"Those are things we just don't know, and we'll have to wait until we get to heaven to find out," she would say. I just couldn't fathom it. The thought intrigued me—such a huge and awesome idea. Sometimes I felt I could almost grasp the concept. I would almost feel dizzy or light-headed if I thought hard enough. A God with no beginning and no ending . . . forever . . . no time, past, present, or future.

I imagined space, out there beyond the stars. Does it have some end to it, this black nothingness? If we could go far enough, would we find the edge of space? And if we did, what might be there?

After Nancie and I had our own children, we would lie out under the stars at night, side by side on the grassy slopes behind our house. We live in the country, where no city lights or streetlights dim the view. On clear, dark summer nights the stars are dazzling and luminous. We've seen brilliant shooting stars streak across the sky, comets with tails, the Milky Way, eclipses of the moon, and space satellites slowly blinking their way along. Sometimes while lying there, I told our children stories that would provoke conversation about God, eternity, and the unknown.

Thoughts about the purpose for life and eternity remain with most of us, always on the edge of our thinking. Am I a random chance being, or was I planned? Is there a reason for life, or is life a cosmic accident? Why am I here? These are fundamental questions that everyone asks. Answers to these questions are often summed up in bumper-sticker phrases. "You only go around once. Grab all the gusto you can get." "Life is just a bowl of cherries." "He who dies with the most toys wins." "Where will you spend eternity?" "What are you leaving future generations?" "Save the planet." "Heaven or hell . . . it's your choice."

For some people, like Martin Luther King Jr., Mother Teresa, or Billy Graham, answering the why-am-I-here questions led them to do incredible things for mankind. For others, like Adolph Hitler, Islamic fundamentalists, or the Oklahoma City bombers, their distorted answers to the why-am-I-here questions led them toward the savage destruction of human life.

Internationally renowned psychiatrist Viktor Frankl, who endured years of unspeakable horror in Nazi death camps, has written an insightful book, *Man's Search for Meaning*. In it he quotes Nietzsche's words: "He who has a *why* to live for can bear with almost any *how*." He goes on to say that the prisoners who survived the awful conditions of the Nazi death camps were the ones who developed a why, an aim for their lives in order to strengthen them to bear the terrible how of their existence. Woe to him who saw no more sense in his life, no aim, no purpose, and, therefore, no point in carrying on. He was soon lost. The typical reply with which such a man rejected all encouraging arguments was, "I have nothing to expect from life any more."[1]

Many people have a weak sense of purpose. They don't spend much time thinking about the goals of their lives. Instead, they've decided just to enjoy the ride and see what happens later. They are called hedonists, and their numbers are increasing.

Hedonists see life as a source of pleasure. Unrestricted sexual pleasure, use of mood-altering substances such as drugs and alcohol, food, and the weekend party become their goals in life. Feeling good is their chief end. For them, the big issues of life include who will win the Super Bowl and the hottest Hollywood movie. And the pursuit of money looms bigger since it is the means to the end. Interestingly, hedonists come from every social strata, every ethnic population, and every age group. Hedonism has its tentacles everywhere.

If our children are to have a sense of purpose, we parents need to ask ourselves what they are learning from us about the meaning of life. Apparently, fewer parents are conveying a true sense of purpose now than they were twenty-five years ago. UCLA's Higher Education Research Institute, which polls the attitudes of the nation's incoming freshmen, has uncovered some revealing facts. In 1966, 84 percent of all incoming freshmen reported that "developing a meaningful philosophy of life" was their most important goal; only 44 percent felt that "being very well off financially" was most important. But by 1990, these proportions had reversed. Only 37 percent felt that a "meaningful philosophy" was the most important life goal; 76 percent answered that "financial success" was their primary aim.[2]

This is the dilemma that our twentysomethings face. Raised with the idea that the chief end of humanity is personal pleasure and affluence, they have become increasingly depressed about the prospects of their future. But who gave them this idea? Wasn't it their baby-boomer parents, the idealists of the sixties, who started out rejecting middle-class affluence but by the time their children were born had embraced affluence and pleasure with a vengeance? But we boomers didn't say it in so many words; we lived it. And in our doing so, it became one of the underlying principles our children adopted into the fiber of their being. My twenty-seven-year-old son recently said to me, "Most of my friends seem to live only for the weekend. They have no other goal in life."

Now the fickle baby-boomer generation is once again in a state of change. A number of national polls show a shift away from the values of self-fulfillment toward the values of family. But this shift is a bit late to influence our twentysomething children who have postponed marriage and family in pursuit of "the weekend." And seeing that the baby boomers have gobbled up most of the high-paying jobs and will not retire for another twenty years, we have a young adult population that has "nothing to expect from life any more."

The problem we are facing is what Paul Hollander of the University of Massachusetts has called a "crisis of meaning." In spite of the fact that we have more exciting options than ever before in the history of mankind, more stuff, more modern gadgets, more communication, more stimulation, and a wide range of comforts, we have little in the way of a *meaning*.[3] We no longer know where we are headed or even why we are headed there.

When NASA launched the first space shuttle, you can bet that they didn't tell the crew, "Let's just fly around for a while and see if we find anything interesting." While this sounds ridiculous, it's exactly what many people do every day by not having a clear understanding of their purpose.

Without a purpose for life that is bigger than we are, we struggle to find meaning. Purpose gives our lives significance. We cannot develop spiritually without a sense of meaning. Life's pain, challenges, and drama are difficult to cope with if we have no meaning. When we have a strong sense of purpose, all experiences, including the painful and difficult ones, bring fulfillment to living. When life has purpose, we do things that matter. When we spend our life doing things that matter, we feel a sense of joy and fulfillment. Only then can we truly enjoy life's pleasures. When we short-circuit the *why* and cut straight to the pleasure, we find life empty and hollow.

Purpose and meaning can be found only when we open our spiritual eyes. Until we seek God, we have no upward vision of the possibilities for hope and direction. Our failure to understand this vital truth has produced millions of people who have gnawing feelings that their lives are out of sync.

Many people have rejected the idea of a sovereign God with a plan for mankind. By doing so, they have cut out the piece of life that solves the puzzle. To cut God out of the equation is to cut away a vital piece of our heart. It leaves little to curb the epidemic of "gimmes" that afflict our kids in this consumer-driven and pleasure-addicted society.

If we want our children to resist the seduction of living life for pleasure rather than meaning, we must provide for them a shared core of spiritual beliefs. When our acts of living are rooted in biblical and religious truths that have proven themselves to be the road maps to wholeness and meaning, our children are able to find their God-given purpose. They can also cope with the inevitable adversity that life will bring. They will have a better chance to stick with their commitments and convictions. Having a *reason* for being provides the strength and stability for all our activities and goals.

⊯ Leading Unexamined Lives
All that is not eternal is eternally out of date.
C. S. LEWIS

TWO OF my friends are a contrast in character. Sam, my "deep" friend, is always thinking about the meaning of things. He examines life *too* much. He spends hours pondering the meaning of life, rarely enjoying it for its beauty and simplicity. He analyzes every person he meets. He does microscopic introspection on his marriage, his job, God, politics, world events, his health, and the depletion of the ozone layer. Sam can't relax. I try to get him to play golf with me, but he considers it a waste of time. I usually feel depressed after being with Sam.

Martin, on the other hand, lives on the surface. His conversation revolves around stuff and events. Sports, cars, trips, and food are his main agenda. He can tell you everything you want to know about the latest improvements in fishing gear or sports cars. He can talk for hours about the best stereo to consider buying. When you try to get him to talk about deeper things, he looks at you blankly and changes the subject to something like the latest player trade of the Portland Trail Blazers. I have never been successful in getting him to talk about what he sees as his calling in life. Martin majors in trivia.

Two real people, two extremes. Most of my friends have more balance. I hope I do too. Unfortunately, I see in the upcoming generation more people leading their lives as Martin does, fewer as Sam does. While most of us do not like to see ourselves living as Sam does, if we don't consider life's deeper meaning, we miss the point of life.

Often we lead, in the words of Patrick Morley, "unexamined lives." In his book *The Man in the Mirror,* Morley makes a convincing case that our compass can be slightly off due to the drift of our culture. He labels the vast majority of Christians "cultural Christians" rather than "biblical Christians." "Cultural Christianity," defines Morley, "means to pursue the God we want instead of the God who is. . . . It is wanting the God we have underlined in our Bibles, without wanting the rest of Him too. It is God relative instead of God absolute."[4]

Sometimes we simply don't stop to consider why we go about life doing what we do. We get so caught up in the process, going to work, watching television, eating out, going to a movie, cleaning the house, washing the car, and living for our vacation, that we simply don't consider what our life's purpose is and what happens when we die.

It seems we have less time to think lofty thoughts, thoughts about character, truth, and cause. Instead we think about what to fix for dinner or what movie we should see. We dwell on immediate gratification, what is urgently calling us. And if we do ponder life, we rarely do it with patience. We want quick solutions, depth in a hurry, truth in a nutshell. We love boiling down the meaning of life into sound bites.

We focus our kids' attention on getting good grades without any thought about the content of the curriculum they are being taught. Good grades are fine, but good grades for what? Meaningless things don't necessarily have to be evil things in order to be meaningless. Much of what we do can be empty. Something is empty when it is practiced without thought or examination. Empty things can be mealtime prayers or working only for a paycheck or watching television.

We do this with our children too. When we tell them to "stop that" or "be quiet," we often do it as a convenience for us, without thinking. We interfere with some of their activity because it annoys us. This does not mean we don't care, but are we caring about the right things? Have we examined what it is we care about? Have we given much thought to what our children are learning and what views of life they are forming under our feet? Have we considered what they might be picking up from us?

Have you considered what your family stands for? Are you "light" to the world, a "city on a mountain, glowing in the night for all to see"?[5] Do your convictions translate into a practiced style of living? Do you express your purpose for being in the way you use your time and energy? Not to consider these things is to lead unexamined lives.

As Naomi Rhode wrote in her book *The Gift of Family,* "Your purpose as a family determines where you live, how you spend your money and your time, your values, and your priorities. The quality of your family life, your relationships with each other, your extended family, and your fellow man are all directly related to your purpose."[6]

It's important to examine our purpose, as individuals and as a family. In the Bible, Gods speaks with disdain for those whom he calls "lukewarm." To be lukewarm means to be neither hot nor cold. In other words, not to have much of an opinion one way or the other is more offensive to God than if you take a position, even if it is the wrong position. To those who lead unexamined lives, God says, "I will spit you out of my mouth!"[7] Harsh words. Something to think about.

What Is My Calling?

One day as Jesus was walking along the shore . . .
he saw two brothers—Simon, also called Peter, and
Andrew—fishing. . . .
Jesus called out to them, "Come, be my disciples,
and I will show you how to fish for people!"
And they left their nets at once and went with him.
MATTHEW 4:18-20

IT HAPPENED in ancient biblical times. Israel was torn in two, warring against itself. The king's son was trying to overthrow his father and take over the kingdom. The main story is about David and his son Absalom. But during the battle an interesting side story develops. It is about the runners who carried messages. In those days, messages were sent by couriers who ran. You had to be a great runner, a fast runner with endurance, to qualify for this job.

Ahimaaz was well qualified. In fact, he may have been the best courier in the land. He had both speed and endurance, and he loved to run.

That day, David's son had been killed in battle. Now this civil war would quickly end. It was time to send word back to David, and a courier was needed. Joab, the captain of David's army, selected a man named Cushi. Joab gave him the official message about the death of Absalom and sent him on his way.

Ahimaaz was heartsick. This was his destiny, to run. He begged Joab to let him run anyway. Joab resisted, but Ahimaaz persisted.

Finally, in frustration, Joab said, "Okay, run!" Joab probably just wanted to get Ahimaaz off his back. Joab no doubt thought that Cushi was so far ahead that Ahimaaz would never catch him anyway.

But Ahimaaz was a fast runner and knew some shortcuts. With several hundred yards to go, he passed Cushi. The king's court saw Ahimaaz coming and waited with anticipation for official word. Ahimaaz, with a grin of satisfaction, ran into the king's court.

King David addresses Ahimaaz and asks him for specific news about the well-being of his son Absalom. Suddenly it dawns on Ahimaaz that he was not assigned to give the message the king is asking to hear. He stammers for a moment and then lamely replies, "When Joab told me to come, there was a lot of shouting; but I didn't know what was happening."

How embarrassing. What a total bust. The king, as he sees Cushi approaching, replies, "Stand aside."

Ahimaaz ran the best race; he finished first. But his race had no purpose. He got his skill and cleverness mixed up with his calling. His calling was to be a courier, a messenger. But he couldn't be a messenger without the message. Running was a needed skill, but the calling was to be the messenger.

I have found myself in similar situations. I get caught up in the competition or engrossed in a project, and the next thing I know, I am asking myself why I am doing what I am doing. Someone said, "All of us are here on this earth with work to do, but our work has nothing to do with our job."[8]

My calling is the essence of who I am. If you want to know my calling, don't ask me how big my business or bank account is or what political party I belong to or whether I would be fun on a fishing trip. Instead, observe what commitments I keep.

I once heard a story about tomatoes. It seems that some farmers in the San Joaquin Valley of California were growing some wonderfully delicious tomatoes. The problem was in the shipping. These vine-ripened beauties did not ship well. By the time they reached the supermarket, most of them were bruised or smashed. What they needed was a tomato that did not bruise so easily. They put some agricultural scientists to work on the problem. Over time, with some genetic manipulation, they developed a gorgeous tomato that could fall off the back of a truck and still suffer no damage. But there was one problem. It didn't taste like a tomato. In the process of becoming bruise proof, it had lost its ability to taste like a tomato.[9] With no flavor, the tomato became just pulp and juice. I think we can agree that the essence of a tomato is first and foremost to taste like a tomato.

I do not want my children to mistake style for substance. I do not want my children to look good on the outside and be empty on the inside. In the flurry of change we live in today, I want them to seek character rather than stuff, to seek truth rather than approval, to seek integrity rather than money, and to seek God rather than success. I want them to find their calling, and once they have found it, I want them to be willing to die for it. I have often told our children that what they become on the outside is not nearly as important to me or to God as what they become on the inside.

I want my children to see their calling as something bigger than their vocation. I have told them that their calling is to be faithful, to keep their commitments, to have integrity, to be compassionate, to find the work that God intends for them to do. I have also told them that their calling will always include something bigger than they are, that it will carry results beyond their lifetime and into the future. G. Campbell Morgan said, "Purpose in life is not to find your freedom but your Master." Fulfilling our calling is what Jesus meant when he encouraged us to "store your treasures in heaven, where they will never become moth-eaten or rusty and where they will be safe from thieves."[10]

🕊 Pursuing God

**As the deer pants for streams of water,
so I long for you, O God.**

PSALM 42:1

THERE was never any doubt when I was growing up about our family's purpose in life. We were a family that possessed a strong evangelical faith. My legacy includes a Christian faith that was rooted in my family before my parents met and married. And although its influence has come and gone, I find a strong Christian faith sprinkled throughout my family history.

Three of my uncles were ordained ministers, and almost all of my aunts, uncles, and cousins regularly attended the same church we did. As far back as I can recall, I was in Sunday school, learning the stories of the Bible. My teachers continually applied these stories to everyday life, emphasizing our purpose. Lillian Hackett, a wide-eyed, smiling, and animated second-grade Sunday school teacher, made the Bible stories come alive for me. Bill Williams, a dedicated youth pastor who later became a missionary, modeled fervency and dedication for me. Earl Book, who took a chance on me when hiring me as an assistant pastor, was a model and mentor in how to seek God.

But the foundation for it all was an underlying purpose in my home. To know God, to accept his grace and forgiveness through Jesus Christ, and to attempt to live our lives in accordance with his Word was the purpose of life. To invest one's life in service and ministry was the highest calling. We had an abiding faith that carried us. When finances were tight, my parents trusted the Word of God, which told them that God was the provider who clothed even the lilies of the field. When my father's bones were broken from an accident and he could not work, he believed that God not only would provide for us but also would bring him back to full health. When I made mistakes, I was told to confess my sins to God and he would forgive me and give me the strength to overcome my temptations and sins.

I was taught that God loves all people and so should I. I was taught that all people are in need of God's grace and forgiveness. I was taught that life on earth is only a prelude to living with God in his kingdom. I was taught that God has no grandchildren, only sons and daughters. My parents let me know that even though my family had this heritage of faith, I had to accept and embrace it for myself.

I was often taught this purpose with Bible stories. One of my favorites was the one found in the New Testament book of Hebrews. The writer uses a powerful analogy of why we all should be living our lives with purpose and vigor. (I can hear my dad telling this story as I write.) He speaks of a great race, an athletic event, in which the runners are running a marathon. They have rounded the corner and entered the great coliseum. There are thousands of fans witnessing this race, cheering and screaming, chanting the racers on toward victory.

The writer-storyteller precedes this analogy with a long list of those who have gone on before, who lived lives of faith and hope, even in the face of almost unbelievable difficulty and heart-stopping peril. He speaks of them proudly, these ancestors who subdued kingdoms, stopped the mouths of lions, quenched the violence of fire, escaped the edge of the sword, waxed valiant in fight, defeated great armies, and even saw their dead raised to life again.

And then he tells his listeners that since there is this huge "cloud of witnesses" who have gone on before us and shown us the way—and are now watching our performance—we should run the race with all that we've got, give it our best shot, resist giving up, and keep our eye on the goal.

From the time I could remember, I was taught these things as a way to visualize and find my purpose in life. We sang songs about it. "A Mighty Fortress Is Our God," "All Hail the Power of Jesus' Name," and "God Leads His Dear Children Along" were three of hundreds of songs that reinforced our sense of God's love and purpose for our lives. Through these stories and songs, I was introduced to the central hope of my legacy, the fact that divine purpose and destiny has come into my family, my bloodline.

When Nancie and I found each other, we discovered that we shared a similar heritage of faith. Nancie and I have attempted to pass this same faith on to our children. It has not always been easy because life is not the same. For one thing, families are not in church as often as they were when we were growing up. Back then, church was a central point of fellowship as well as teaching. We were there several times each week for fellowships, Bible studies, and other activities. Today, Sunday school attendance has dropped dramatically and continues to drop in some denominations as much as 6 percent a year. That is alarming when you realize that nothing has come along to take its place.

More and more of the responsibility to pass on our faith and purpose to our children has fallen to us parents. And this at a time when we have more choices and options to confuse and clutter our lives. I know that it is vital to me and my family to make the pursuit of God a top priority. I do not offer simple solutions because I know it takes personal resolve to give up other things to make time for this. I simply say that if we parents do not make pursuing God a priority, it will not happen for our families.

When we model this commitment to our children, they will have a clearer vision of God. With the pursuit of God comes a clear vision of purpose. The teachings on the fruit of the Spirit—love, joy, peace, patience, kindness, goodness, faithfulness, gentleness, and self-control—take on meaning when we understand our purpose for being.[11] Living our lives with integrity makes sense when the purpose is clear.

Faith gives us reasons to live moral lives. It gives us hope to endure hardship. It gives us powerful motivation to love each other. It gives us strength by binding us together. It sets the agenda for a social order that creates peace and happiness among its followers. It has a history that records the benefits of its virtues. Faith gives purpose texture and color, a plan that leads us home.

When we introduce our children to God, we are teaching them that there is a higher power to which we are all accountable. Children begin to understand that the authority and guidelines given by their parents come from universal moral absolutes, not just Mom and Dad.

ℒ Seeing Miracles Happen

Prayer is [the] way of declaring that
the boundaries of life and the limits of hope
cannot be drawn with the crayons of time and space.
ANTHONY PADAVANO

IT WAS in the bedroom I shared with my younger brother in our little house on Rutland Avenue in San Jose, California, that I first noticed it. I was seven years old. The house was small: two bedrooms, one bathroom, a tiny kitchen with a Formica-topped table, a small living room, and a back porch, where my older sister slept.

You could almost hear a whisper through the paper-thin walls. I often went to sleep at night hearing my parents talking in the kitchen or laughing with friends in the living room or whispering in their bedroom.

But now, for the first time, I was not just hearing . . . I was listening. I listened to my father praying. "O God, we love you and want you to be the Lord of our lives. We pray for our children, dear Lord." As I listened I heard my name. "And for Billy we pray that you will, even at this age, begin to speak to his heart about following you. We pray that you will give us wisdom in raising this boy. We pray that you will wrap your loving and protecting arms around him and that your heavenly angels will watch over him."

Somehow I knew I was witness to the sacred. I knew this was the Holy of Holies. I knew what I was hearing was my father's faith, out of the Sunday service and into his everyday life. I knew this was real. His prayer had a profound effect on me. I knew from then on that I was under some kind of special protection and direction. My own spiritual significance began to take on meaning for me from that moment.

Now, forty-five years later, I can still hear the wonderful voice of my father in prayer. I have heard it thousands of times, but I never tire of hearing it again. My father is now eighty-four. Recently he called me and asked where I was going to speak that week and then ended the conversation by saying, "I'll be praying for you." Last summer I had the chance to take my father on a fishing trip. Just after we turned out the lights, we prayed together. It was as if I were his small child again, hearing that wonderful voice in earnest prayer to God.[12]

Teaching our children to pray is teaching them how to link up with almighty God. Teaching them to pray and praying for them is the greatest gift we can give our children. Prayer is the powerful force that makes miracles happen and gives power to our lives.

We parents spend a lot of time worrying about what kind of world we are leaving our children. Maybe it's time to be more concerned about what kind of inner strength and traits of godliness are left to our children. After all, we cannot change world conditions, but we can influence our children.

As I pray for my children, I realize my own weaknesses, and I begin to seek God's help for my own life. Prayer also makes me more conscious of the attitudes of my family. As insight into each of my children's unique gifts emerges, I am able to help them clarify and encourage God's gifts within them: Jonathan's strong gift of influence and leadership; Eric's often hidden spirit of tenderness and compassion; Chris's heartfelt sense of justice and honor; Andy's wonderful warmth, smile, and gift of hospitality; and Amy's deep sense of compassion for the poor and downtrodden.

In the end, to be what some call a "prayer warrior" is a pretty good legacy.

✒ Giving Children a Sense of Mission

To some this world may seem like no place to bring up a child. And in some respects they are right. But we take that risk anyway with the comforting knowledge that it is not for this world that we prepare them.

KAREN L. TORNBERG

LIFE'S mission can take on many forms. Missions are tasks, given by God, as an outgrowth of our calling. If we are called to help the poor, our mission might be to establish a food-distribution center in the Bronx. If we enter into a marriage, our mission is to love, honor, and cherish our spouse until death separates us. A mission is an assignment with a specific objective in mind. In fact, our calling and all of our commitments are accompanied by a mission.

Parents fit in this category. The little lives that have been placed in our care need specific things from us. They need food, shelter, and clothing. They need love, care, and attention. They need teaching, example, and discipline. Most important, they need to be shown the eternal purpose of life. Our mission as parents should be to raise our children in the best way we know how, constantly improving our skills.

One day we decided to write a "statement of mission" for our family. Corporations do this all the time. They decide why they exist as a company, what the company has been called to accomplish, and they write it down in a sentence or two. It has been vital to most corporations for every key player in the company to know the mission statement. This is what we have come to see is our family's mission statement:

Our mission as a family is

- To love God above all else and be obedient to his Word
- To love each other, building up rather than diminishing each other
- To help each other discover our God-given gifts and calling
- To celebrate whenever and wherever we can
- To reach out to others with our time and resources in ways that build God's kingdom
- To pray continuously for each other and those around us
- To strive for excellence in whatever we do

God calls us to a diligent task of raising our children with purpose. It is an awesome task filled with joy and pain. But it is worth the risk and the effort. In fact, our purpose as parents is to fulfill God's call to bring up our children in healthy homes, good ground.

Your children are living treasures, deposited into your account by almighty God. They will live their lives, in part, by the road map you give them. They will touch thousands of others through their lives—their spouses, their children, their friends, their coworkers. They may even influence a nation with their God-given gifts.

Much of the core of who they are and what they will deposit in others is being formed in them at home. They draw nutrients from the ground you, as parents, provide. It is an awesome responsibility, but as writer Kate Douglas Wiggin said, "Somewhere is the child who will write the novel that will stir hearts to nobler issues and incite them to better deeds. There is the child who will paint the greatest picture or carve the greatest statue of the age; who will deliver his country in an hour of peril; give his life for a great principle; another born more of the spirit than of the flesh who will live continually on the heights of moral being and in dying will draw others to morality. It may be that I shall preserve one of these children to the race. It is a peg big enough on which to hang a hope. For every child is a new incarnate thought of God, an ever fresh and radiant possibility."[13]

TILLING THE GROUND
Questions for Thought and Reflection

As you think about how you can practice the habit of making your home a place of purpose, record your thoughts in a journal or notebook. Then share your reflections with your spouse or a close friend, asking them to pray for you and help you to put into practice some of the things about which you have been convicted.

1. What is your purpose in life?
2. Are your children aware of that purpose? How do you communicate that purpose?
3. What people and experiences influenced your life goals?
4. What are the threats to living out your life purpose? What can you do to lessen those threats?
5. What experiences can you give your children to help them discover life's purposes?
6. What people will have significant impact on your children and their life purposes? How can you encourage and support those people?
7. What is your spouse's purpose in life?

8. Are your children aware of that purpose? How do they see you encouraging and affirming your spouse's purpose?

9. What is your family's spoken or unspoken mission statement?

10. How can you make your home a place in which your family can live out that mission?

11. What do you feel is God's purpose for your life? How does that fit with your own purpose? How are you living out God's purpose for your life?

12. What do you think is God's purpose for your family? How are you living out that purpose?

CHAPTER 9
Spring Again

God's ways are as hard to discern as the pathways of the wind,
and as mysterious as a tiny baby
being formed in a mother's womb.
Be sure to stay busy and plant a variety of crops,
for you never know which will grow—
perhaps they all will.

ECCLESIASTES 11:5-6

This past spring I went back to my brother-in-law's farm. It was the first time in a long time that I have been back to the farm in spring. Something about spring makes my heart fill with joy and expectation. The earth, awakening from a deep, cold slumber, is coming to life again. New nests, new shoots of green, new hope. Spring is testimony that God is a God of second chances—for the earth, for farmers, and for families.

APRIL 1

It's spring again! I arrived back at the farm at three o'clock in the morning after driving all night. Dan was hoping to start planting two weeks ago, but the ground is still too wet. Snow lies in patches everywhere.

But the sun was warm and streaming through my window when I awoke this morning. It was almost ten o'clock. It's beautiful this morning. It's been warm, almost hot, for the past five days. I shuffled downstairs and poured a cup of coffee. The house was empty, but Dan's wife, Nancy, left a slice of coffee cake with a note. "Welcome back! I had to run to town. I'll be back by noon."

I walked out past the barn and looked out across the field. A slow column of dust rose off to the east from where I heard the faraway drone of Dan's tractor as he plowed. Golden-breasted meadowlarks sang nearby. Swallows circled the barn, darting in and out of their mud nests. Sparrows brought bits of string and straw to the cracks and eaves hiding their nests. It's as if the whole earth is beckoning with the hope of trying again.

APRIL 2

The winter has been long, harsh at times, as storms swept across the rolling fields. But now it's April! The Rocky Mountains off to the west somehow look closer, gentler, and the glaciers glisten with fresh snow. The trees around the house have begun to leaf out. Soon dandelions will bring cheery splashes of yellow.

Today, my assignment was to go out into the fields and pick up rocks. Too many rocks choke the grain Dan will soon plant. I have done this before. It's hard work. I bounced along in the old flatbed pickup this afternoon, finding big boulders to remove. As I heaved them up onto the bed of the truck, I kept wondering why they keep turning up from somewhere deep in the earth. Each year more rocks appear. Where do they come from?

The rocks remind me of my own life. No matter how much picking and cleaning I try to do, it seems that more rocks surface and need to be dealt with. I'm glad God knows that and never gives up on me.

APRIL 3

Dan has been plowing and planting for nearly a week now. Spring plowing–summer fallowing Dan calls it–used to be more of a dirty business than it is today. Now Dan has an enclosed, air-conditioned cab with stereos and earphones.

I notice Dan is more cheerful in the spring too, in spite of the hard winter. "Lots of snow leaves good moisture in the ground," he says. "Spring changes my whole attitude. It makes me feel ornery again!" he jokes. My farmer in-laws seem to have a special feeling about spring–the breaking up of hard ground, the preparation of the soil to receive the seed. Spring means promise, hope. Forget the hail that wiped out last year's crop. Here is a fresh start, a new chance at harvest.

APRIL 4

It is amazing to me how one tiny seed can produce so much more than itself. The partnership between the soil, the seed, and the farmer is an awesome thing. It is a marriage of sorts. How the ground must welcome it! Together their fruits feed thousands. Together, their bounty sustains life.

In the bag, the seed lies dormant. It has potential for life, but without the nutrients of soil and rain, it remains dead. It takes cooperation for life to happen. The seed plus good ground, moisture, sun, and the loving care of a never-quit farmer combine to make it happen.

Growth doesn't come without struggle. Between now and harvest, Dan will battle weeds, aphids, cutworms, wireworms, grasshoppers, and gophers, not to mention the ever present threat of drought or hail.

IT'S THAT way with families too. When the precious seeds God gives us are planted in good ground, growth happens in our homes. But growth does not come without diligence, dedication, and suffering. We must till the ground, pick the rocks, battle the pests, and pray. Earl Book, my spiritual mentor, once said to me, "Bill, there is no success without suffering. Either you will suffer, or someone will suffer for you if you experience success."

I hope that this book has helped you see that raising good children and having a healthy home are matters of being, not doing. Good ground is a matter of the heart, not the head, a matter of faith, not formula. The fact that you have read this book indicates that you are a parent who really cares about your children. You are a person who wants to grow and leave a rich legacy to your children. One small seed can produce so much. A few seeds make a garden. After that, who knows? God is faithful to provide that harvest if we do our part. Keep adding those rich nutrients to the soil of your home.

In the end, it's the soil, the environment of home, that makes it happen. *Refuge* provides the place and lets us know we're safe. *Formation* provides the virtues and gives us tools to become. *Boundaries* provide the context and let us know the rules. *Celebration* provides the joy and lets us know life is good. *Connection* provides belonging and lets us know we're loved. *Legacy* provides the roots and lets us know from whence we came. *Purpose* provides the reason and lets us discover our calling.

Seeds are amazing things when they are planted in good ground. May the Lord of the harvest bless you as you tend the good ground of your home and provide a safe place for your children to grow.

It's spring again! Go for it!

ABOUT THE AUTHOR

BILL CARMICHAEL has spent most of his adult life working to build healthy families, including his own family of five children. Bill has been a counselor, teacher, youth pastor, pastor, writer, editor, and publisher; his wife, Nancie, has been the editor of *Virtue* magazine for sixteen years and continues to write "The Deeper Life" column for *Virtue.* Bill and Nancie are the founding publishers of Good Family Magazines, which include *Virtue, Christian Parenting Today,* and *Parents of Teenagers.* Bill and Nancie have written three books, including Tyndale's *Lord, Bless My Child.* The Carmichaels live in Black Butte Ranch, Oregon.

NOTES

Chapter 2: Refuge: Am I Safe?
1. Robert Frost, "The Death of the Hired Man."
2. John 14:1-3.
3. *Baseball,* PBS special eight-volume video series, tape no. 8, Turner Home Entertainment.
4. Henri Nouwen, *The Return of the Prodigal Son* (New York: Doubleday, 1992), 37.
5. Annette LaPlaca, ed., *Read It on the Refrigerator* (Wheaton, Ill.: Shaw, 1992), 23.
6. Proverbs 15:1.
7. Bob Benson Sr., *Disciplines for the Inner Life* (Nashville: Thomas Nelson, 1989), 294.
8. Taken from *Treasures of Inspiration,* calendar (Fort Worth, Tex.: Brownlow, 1992).
9. Psalm 90:1; 91:1-5, 11, NIV.

Chapter 3: Formation: Who Am I?
1. John Powell, *Fully Human, Fully Alive* (Niles, Ill.: Argus Communications, 1976), 65.
2. Quoted in William J. Bennett, *The De-Valuing of America* (New York: Summit Books, 1992), 23.
3. Phyllis Theroux, *Night Lights* (New York: Viking, 1987), 35.
4. Isaiah 53:6.
5. Proverbs 29:18, KJV.
6. Bennett, *The De-Valuing of America,* 21.
7. Allan Bloom, *The Closing of the American Mind* (New York: Simon & Schuster, 1987), 239.
8. Taken from *Treasures of Inspiration,* calendar (Fort Worth, Tex.: Brownlow, 1992).

9. Gwen Weising, *A Working Woman's Guide to Joy,* calendar (Minneapolis: Garborg's, 1994).
10. Laura Schlessinger, *How Could You Do That?* (New York: HarperCollins, 1996), 12.
11. Jack Schreur and Jerry Schreur, *Family Fears* (Wheaton, Ill.: Victor Books, 1994), 38.
12. James Dobson, *Hide or Seek* (Old Tappan, N.J.: Fleming H. Revell, 1990), 44.
13. William J. Bennett, *The Book of Virtues* (New York: Simon & Schuster, 1993), 347.
14. Ibid.
15. Acts 20:34-35.
16. Joan Chittister, "Work: Participation in Creation," *Weavings* (Jan./Feb. 1993): 10.
17. Ibid.
18. Quoted in Bennett, *The Book of Virtues,* 85.
19. Charles Swindoll, *The Quest for Character* (Portland, Ore.: Multnomah, 1987), 171.
20. Quoted in Frederic Brussat and Mary Ann Brussat, *100 Ways to Keep Your Soul Alive* (San Francisco: Harper San Francisco, 1994), 50.
21. Girt S. Disney, "Feasts in the Desert and Other Unlikely Places," *Weavings* (Jan./Feb. 1994): 45.

Chapter 4: Boundaries: What Are the Rules?

1. Henry Cloud and John Townsend, *Boundaries: When to Say Yes, When to Say No, to Take Control of Your Life* (Grand Rapids: Zondervan, 1992), 29.
2. Ibid., 33–38.
3. Ron Taffel with Melinda Blau, *Parenting by Heart* (Reading, Mass.: Addison-Wesley, 1991), 9.
4. Cloud and Townsend, *Boundaries,* 26.
5. Valerie Bell, *Getting Out of Your Kids' Faces & into Their Hearts* (Grand Rapids: Zondervan, 1994), 115.
6. Ibid.
7. Ibid., 42.
8. Quoted in Charles Swindoll, *Simple Faith* (Waco, Tex.: Word, 1991), 244.
9. Carol Kuykendall, *Give Them Wings* (Colorado Springs, Colo.: Focus on the Family, 1994), 34.
10. John K. Rosemond, "The Three R's of Self-Esteem," *Hemispheres* (Jan. 1993): 76.
11. Quoted in ibid.
12. Ibid.
13. Jeff Van Vonderen, *Families Where Grace Is in Place* (Minneapolis: Bethany House, 1992), 165.

14. Polly Berrien Berends, *Gently Lead* (New York: HarperCollins, 1991), 60.
15. Quoted in *Mother,* calendar (Minneapolis: Garborg's, 1995).
16. Phyllis Theroux, *Night Lights* (New York: Viking, 1987), 109.
17. Quoted in Jack Canfield and Mark Victor Hansen, *Chicken Soup for the Soul* (Dearfield Beach, Fla.: Health Communications, Inc., 1993), 119.

Chapter 5: Celebration: Is Life Good?
1. Quoted in William Carmichael and Nancie Carmichael, *Lord, Bless My Child* (Wheaton, Ill.: Tyndale, 1995), 133.
2. Luke 2:10.
3. John 15:11.
4. Richard Foster, *Celebration of Discipline: The Path to Spiritual Growth* (San Francisco: Harper San Francisco, 1988), 191.
5. Laurie Beth Jones, *Jesus, CEO: Using Ancient Wisdom for Visionary Leadership* (New York: Hyperion, 1995), 32.
6. Joyce Maynard, "Hopes and Prayers," *Parenting* (May 1994): 51.
7. Quoted in Jack Canfield and Mark Victor Hansen, *Chicken Soup for the Soul* (Dearfield Beach, Fla.: Health Communications, Inc., 1993), 12.
8. Mark 10:14.
9. Quoted in Cheryl Forbes, *Imagination* (Portland, Ore.: Multnomah, 1986), 9.
10. Ibid., 19.
11. Ibid.
12. Lewis B. Smedes, *Shame and Grace* (San Francisco: Harper San Francisco, 1993), 164.
13. Quoted in Elisa Morgan, *What Every Mom Needs* (Grand Rapids: Zondervan, 1995), 173.
14. Quoted in ibid., 172.
15. Annette LaPlaca, ed., *Read It on the Refrigerator* (Wheaton, Ill.: Shaw, 1992), 39.
16. Paul Pearsall, *The Power of the Family* (New York: Doubleday, 1990), 39.
17. Jeremiah 31:21.

Chapter 6: Connection: Am I Loved?
1. Paul Pearsall, *The Power of the Family* (New York: Doubleday, 1990), 21.
2. "Finally, a Judge Recognizes the Tragedy," *Chicago Tribune,* 21 Apr. 1996.
3. Lewis B. Smedes, *Shame and Grace* (San Francisco: Harper San Francisco, 1993), 71.
4. Joanna Powell, *Things I Should Have Said to My Father* (New York: Avon Books, 1994), 71.
5. Bob Keeshan, *Growing Up Happy* (New York: Doubleday, 1991), 17.
6. Josh McDowell and Dick Day, *Why Wait?* (San Bernadino, Calif.: Here's Life Publishers, 1988), 388.

7. David Augsburger, *Caring Enough to Confront* (Scottdale, Pa.: Herald, 1980).
8. Paul Tournier, *To Understand Each Other* (Atlanta: John Knox Press, 1967), 8.
9. Ibid., 61.
10. Stephen R. Covey, *The 7 Habits of Highly Effective People* (New York: Simon & Schuster, 1989), 239.
11. John Bradshaw, *Bradshaw On: The Family* (Dearfield Beach, Fla.: Health Communications, Inc., 1988), 52.
12. Nick Stinnett and John DeFrain, "Six Secrets of Strong Families," *Reader's Digest* (Nov. 1994): 132–135.
13. Pearsall, *The Power of the Family*, 4.
14. *Christianity Today* (27 Aug. 1976).
15. Ross Campbell, *How to Really Love Your Child* (Wheaton, Ill.: Victor Books, 1982), 60–61.
16. M. Scott Peck, *The Road Less Traveled* (New York: Simon & Schuster, 1978), 23–24.
17. Quoted in Alfred H. Ells, *Family Love* (Nashville: Thomas Nelson, 1990), 39.
18. Allan Bloom, *The Closing of the American Mind* (New York: Simon & Schuster, 1987), 119.
19. Quoted in William Kilpatrick, *Why Johnny Can't Tell Right from Wrong* (New York: Simon & Schuster, 1992), 264.
20. Max Depree, *Leadership Is an Art* (New York: Doubleday, 1989), 71.
21. Matthew 25:34-36.
22. James 1:27.
23. Gary Smalley, *The Key to Your Child's Heart* (Waco, Tex.: Word, 1984), 162.

Chapter 7: Legacy: Where Do I Belong?
1. Katharine M. Jones, *Heroines of Dixie* (New York: Smithmark Publishers, 1995), 78.
2. Ibid.
3. Garrison Keillor, *Leaving Home* (New York: Viking Penguin, 1987), xix.
4. M. Scott Peck, *In Search of Stones* (New York: Hyperion, 1995), 159.
5. Elizabeth Berg, *Family Traditions* (New York: Reader's Digest Association, 1992), 12.
6. Robert Fulghum, *From Beginning to End: The Rituals of Our Lives* (New York: Villard Books, 1995), 200.
7. Quoted in Sue Monk Kidd, "The Story Shaped Life," *Weavings* (Jan./Feb. 1989): 21.
8. Michael E. Williams, "Voices from Unseen Rooms and Community," *Weavings* (July/Aug., 1990): 34.
9. Kidd, "The Story Shaped Life," 21.
10. William Kilpatrick, *Why Johnny Can't Tell Right from Wrong* (New York: Simon & Schuster, 1992), 208.

11. Lewis B. Smedes, *Shame and Grace* (San Francisco: Harper San Francisco, 1993), 70.
12. Lewis B. Smedes, *A Pretty Good Person* (San Francisco: Harper & Row, 1990), 23.
13. David Kopp, *Christian Parenting Today* (Mar./Apr. 1993): 6.

Chapter 8: Purpose: Why Am I Here?

1. Viktor Frankl, *Man's Search for Meaning* (New York: Washington Square Press, 1984), 9.
2. David Lipsky and Alexander Abrams, *Late Bloomers* (New York: Times Books-Random House, 1994), 32.
3. Quoted in John Liscio, *U.S. News & World Report* (29 June 1992): 65.
4. Patrick Morley, *The Man in the Mirror* (Nashville: Wolgemuth & Hyatt, 1989), 33.
5. Matthew 5:14.
6. Naomi Rhode, *The Gift of Family* (Nashville: Thomas Nelson, 1991), 21.
7. Revelation 3:16.
8. Barbara De Angelis, *Real Moments* (New York: Dell, 1994), 117.
9. Illustration borrowed from a talk given by Lewis Smedes at an Evangelical Christian Publishers Association in 1984 in Palm Springs, California.
10. Matthew 6:20.
11. Galatians 5:22-23.
12. This story was first shared in print in the introduction to Nancie's and my book *Lord, Bless My Child* (Wheaton, Ill.: Tyndale, 1995).
13. Kate Douglas Wiggin, quoted in Alice Lawson Sperapani, "The Christmas Conneciton," *Virtue* (Nov./Dec. 1995): 51.